SCHOOL CRISIS SURVIVAL GUIDE

Management Techniques and Materials for Counselors and Administrators

Suni Petersen
Ronald L. Straub

THE CENTER FOR APPLIED
RESEARCH IN EDUCATION
West Nyack, New York 10995

Library of Congress Cataloging-in-Publication Data

Petersen, Suni, 1944– .
    School crisis survival guide : management techniques and materials
for counselors and administrators / Suni Petersen, Ronald L. Straub.
        p.   cm.
    Includes bibliographical references and index.
    ISBN 0-87628-806-9
    1. School psychology—United States.   2. Crisis management—United
States—Planning.   3. Crisis intervention (Psychology)—United
States—Planning.   I. Straub, Ronald L., 1943–   .   II. Title.
    LB1027.55.P47   1992   91-21679
    371.4'6—dc20   CIP

Printed in the United States of America

10   9   8

ISBN 0-87628-806-9

**THE CENTER FOR APPLIED RESEARCH
IN EDUCATION**
West Nyack, NY 10994
A Simon & Schuster Company

On the World Wide Web at http://www.phdirect.com

Prentice-Hall International (UK) Limited, *London*
Prentice-Hall of Australia Pty. Limited, *Sydney*
Prentice-Hall Canada Inc., *Toronto*
Prentice-Hall Hispanoamericana, S.A., *Mexico*
Prentice-Hall of India Private Limited, *New Delhi*
Prentice-Hall of Japan, Inc., *Tokyo*
Simon & Schuster Asia Pte. Ltd., *Singapore*
Editora Prentice-Hall do Brasil, Ltda., *Rio de Janeiro*

Acknowledgments

Although we are the authors of this book, we are not the authors of every idea presented. These guidelines have many authors. This book is a compilation of actions gleaned from the experience of the authors, the educators participating in innumerable workshops and the hindsight of crisis team debriefings.

However, certain people who shared their ideas and experience deserve special acknowledgment:

Gary Alderman — *School Psychology Supervisor—Charleston, South Carolina Schools*

Kitty Aultman — *Student Services Director—Charleston, South Carolina Schools*

Carolyn Broughton — *Jacksonville, Florida Motion Picture Liaison, Office Information Services*

Michael Crews — *News Director—Jacksonville, Florida*

Karen Dunne-Maxim — *Coordinator Suicide Prevention Project, University of Medicine and Dentistry of New Jersey*

Patricia Howard — *School Psychology Supervisor—Duval County Public Schools*

Several principals, counselors, and superintendents requested anonymity to protect the confidentiality of their students and schools.

We wish to thank these dedicated people for their contributions to this work.

We also wish to thank our unofficial computer specialist, James Craggs, for tolerating countless interruptions in his life.

DEDICATION

To my children, Lee, Greg and Kevin, with gratitude for the richness they bring to my life and to my husband, Ron, my greatest supporter, confidant and cohort in creative challenge.

Suni Petersen

To my wife, who is my best friend, and her three sons, whom I love as my own.

Ronald L. Straub

About the Authors

SUNI PETERSEN has seven years' experience designing prevention programs for schools, and has trained sixteen southeastern school systems how to plan for crises. She has also made three videos on grief and crisis for the Florida State Department of Education, and serves as a member of the Critical Incident Stress Debriefing Team for the Duval County (Florida) police, fire, and rescue squads.

A licensed mental health counselor, Ms. Petersen has been a practicing family therapist for thirteen years. She developed her expertise in crisis and death counseling through her work with seriously and terminally ill clients and families in crisis and grief at Hospice Northeast in Florida. Most recently, she created a program called "Even Angels Need Love," which seeks to prevent burnout of professional medical staff by providing support and professional development. This program has been conducted at hospices and hospitals throughout Florida and profiled in *Caring Journal*. Ms. Petersen also co-authored, with Frances Wiggins, a workbook and manual on stress management.

Ms. Petersen received her Bachelors' and Masters' degrees from the University of North Florida. She is a member of the Florida Association for Counseling and Development, The National Organization for Victim Assistance, The National Hospice Organization, and the National Association of Mental Health Counselors. Ms. Petersen has three sons and enjoys creating hand-dyed silk wall hangings and wearable art.

RONALD L. STRAUB was born in Wisconsin and educated at Holy Cross Seminary in LaCrosse, Wisconsin, and St. John's University in Collegeville, Minnesota. He has a Bachelors' degree in Philosophy and a Masters' degree in Divinity. As a Catholic priest, he taught high school, provided support to the dying in an oncology hospital, and worked as a counselor in a parish. After leaving the priesthood, Mr. Straub moved to St. Augustine, Florida, and continued counseling, focusing on drug and alcohol addiction. He has since turned his attention to woodworking and writing. He has written national advertising copy and scripted various training videos and audio tapes.

Ron and Suni are married and live in St. Augustine. Many of their projects and writings are joint efforts.

About This Resource

Schools today are often confronted by an incredible array of attitudes, cultural differences, and emotional and social upheavals. It is a challenge just to function effectively, on a day-to-day basis. When a crisis strikes, even the most capable staff can quickly become overwhelmed. Educators usually have not been trained to handle the types of crises that are occurring with increasing frequency in schools. Even traumas that occur away from school ultimately affect behavior in the classroom. Drawn from the personal experience of the authors and many educators who have encountered crisis situations, the *School Crisis Survival Guide* offers you practical and realistic support in developing an effective plan *before* a crisis strikes your school, as well as in adapting and implementing your plan once it does.

Crisis As Opportunity

The Chinese have a symbol representing crisis. It is comprised of two characters: "wei," meaning *danger,* and "ji," meaning *opportunity.* The former describes a crisis; the latter predicts its potential. The "danger" of a crisis is that it can be devastating. The effects can be debilitating and long-term. This is what you seek to avoid. The effects can also be growth-producing, bringing about permanent, positive change. In a crisis, the very foundations upon which an individual has built his or her life are leveled, presenting the "opportunity" to rebuild a more substantial foundation. This book is meant to be used as a tool to help ensure that potentially

devastating crises, both individual and group, will become opportunities for health and growth within your schools.

Why Address Crisis in the School?

Crisis situations are caused by specific events: a tornado, an explosion, an unexpected death, a terrorist act, an automobile accident. They can also be more individualized, resulting from divorces, separations, family fights or abuse. They will push persons out of control. Crises disrupt the flow of everyday life and take the individual by surprise. Fear of the unknown forcefully presents itself: *What will happen now? What will happen to me? Will I survive? Maybe I'll die!* Whatever the cause, some form of personal and perhaps social pandemonium will follow. Without a specific plan of action designed to deal with a crisis, an already distressful condition can and probably will get worse before it gets better.

HOW TO USE THIS BOOK

The *School Crisis Survival Guide* offers you detailed guidelines and materials for putting together an effective crisis management plan at both the school and the school-system level. However, since each school and each critical incident is unique in nature, you must adapt the guidelines we offer to fit your school and its particular crisis.

The Five Parts of the Guide

Before developing your plan, you must select and assemble a team of qualified individuals from your staff. The background information and guidelines needed to develop your crisis team are presented in Part I, *Planning for Crisis.* The functions of the team and responsibilities of each member are spelled out in detail. At the end of Part I a detailed checklist is provided to guide you through the preparation of your own crisis management plan and the organization of vital information you need to have on hand.

After your team is assembled, the step-by-step guidelines in Part II, *The Crisis Team in Motion,* will assist you in developing your plan, educating your staff, and establishing community contacts so that you will be prepared to handle any crisis when it strikes.

Part III, *Crisis Counseling,* provides information and techniques for crisis and grief counseling for children at various stages of development, as well as information about Post Traumatic Stress Disorder and how to prevent it.

Part IV, *Activities for the Resolution of Trauma and Grief* provides 32 individual, group and class activities for various ages that can be used to help restore emotional health. There are also beginner's guidelines for leading groups.

Because suicide, violence and natural disasters all require specific responses, Part V, *Special Concerns for Specific Crises* covers the unique problems of various crises and includes steps for the prevention of suicide and violence. In Part IV you will also learn about factors that increase the likelihood of trauma in any crisis. This section concludes with recommendations for dealing with a dying child in the classroom.

The GUIDE concludes with two useful appendices: an extensive list of books for students at various levels, and a list of useful resources for educators.

The *School Crisis Survival Guide* will train you to help children not only to survive crises, but also to grow and learn from them. It will enable you to help your students (and your staff) put traumatic events in perspective, and it will assist both you and them in acquiring a deeper appreciation of the value of life.

Suni Petersen
Ronald L. Straub

Contents

PART V. SPECIAL CONCERNS FOR SPECIFIC CRISES 137

PLANNING FOR CRISIS

Introduction

A CRISIS IS an event that is extraordinary and therefore cannot be predicted. The human reactions to a crisis, however, are consistent and very predictable. Being aware of and understanding beforehand how people will react in a critical situation make it possible to implement a plan that defuses those reactions and prevents them from precipitating a secondary crisis.

In Part I, we will review the foundations of a plan for managing a school crisis:

- acknowledging the need
- recognizing and assigning responsibilities
- defining the components of a good plan
- establishing your own crisis team.

WHAT CONSTITUTES A CRISIS?

Some examples might help:

*   *   *

Eight-year-old Sarah was an angry child of divorcing parents. Her classmates were often provoked into fights by her sarcasm. Sarah was in a small plane along with her mother and grandparents when it crashed, killing them all. The children in her school were caught in a web of shock and mixed emotions.

*   *   *

Mark, Sandy, Rebecca and Steve left a party early one Saturday night and crashed while speeding down a winding road. There were no survivors.

*   *   *

Principal Dave Anderson approached his school early one morning to find the body of a student hanging from the bleachers: a suicide.

*   *   *

A fire started in the library of the high school on Saturday. Over one-third of the building was burned and students needed to be assigned to three other schools.

*   *   *

A second grade teacher's ex-husband rushed into her classroom and shot her in front of the class.

*   *   *

Two students left the school riding a bicycle. They were never heard from again. The abandoned bicycles were found a block away from the school.

*   *   *

A tornado tore through a town, clearing a path 100 yards wide. Several people were killed and many houses were demolished.

WHY THE SCHOOL MUST ADDRESS A CRISIS

Because we live in a society that is becoming increasingly complex and volatile, it is essential to develop a crisis plan within the school system. When school personnel are prepared to deal with crisis, students can continue to grow emotionally, intellectually and physically. Divisiveness and further trauma can be averted. With proper preparation, a crisis can then be used to unite students and staff in building confidence and cohesiveness among themselves and within the larger public community. A closer look at what the school is should help to emphasize its essential and inherent role in resolving crisis.

Serving the Wider Community

The school is incredibly influential in the daily lives of each family within the community. Much of the nurturing and discipline needed in raising a son or daughter centers on their performance and behavior in school. Even those parents who are not active in the school's organization have a silent interest and investment in their children's school environment. The school thus becomes an integral and effective force within the life of each family and of the community as a whole.

Nowhere was this more evident than in the elementary school most affected by the *Starke* attack. In 1987, the *USS Starke* was attacked in the Persian Gulf by the Iranians. When President Reagan flew to the Mayport Naval Base in Florida to speak at a memorial service for the deceased, security was very tight and many local people were denied entry to the base. A similar service was also conducted by the elementary school, since several of its students had suffered the loss of a parent in the *Starke* attack. Unexpectedly, the service was attended by four hundred adults from the community. The school, unknowingly, had provided an essential service to members of the larger community who needed, for whatever reasons, to express their grief.

Substituting for the Extended Family

In traditional American communities before the 1950s, the nuclear family received support from a geographically close extended family. When children needed someone other than parents to speak with, grandparents or an uncle or aunt were usually available. When parents faced hardships, for example, death or unemployment, the extended family provided a ready support system well acquainted with the needs and temperament of the individuals'.

Population growth and job mobility changed the traditional family. New communities were created, inhabited by people devoid of a shared history and deprived of the strength offered by the extended family. Intergenerational wisdom was no longer available on demand. The mobile family of today tends to adopt the community in which it happens to find itself. The school in that community thus plays a role in the children's and family's life never before expected from an educational institution.

The school today is expected to address not only the intellectual, but also the emotional, social, and physical needs of the student. More and more, parents are looking to the schools for the back-up support previously offered by the extended family.

Providing Services to Children

It takes time to resolve a trauma. An experience such as a student hanging himself, a classmate killed by a drunk driver, a shooting in the school or the death of a loved mentor and teacher is not resolved in three days.

Calling on a community psychologist to come into the school for a few days during a crisis is a good practice because additional resources help to accommodate the workload. However, the work with the students must continue after the community psychologist returns to his or her office. It is the school, then, that remains the constant and consistent support system for the students.

After the first few days of a crisis, the number of students needing help will have decreased substantially, but some will still need counseling to prevent Post Traumatic Stress Disorder, and this follow-up counseling is different from that usually associated with the guidance department. Timely, quick interventions can prove to be a far more effective means to recovery than spending hours in a psychologist's office every Thursday afternoon. A well-trained staff, sensitized to the particular needs of the students during a crisis, *can* provide this service.

Maintaining a Cohesive School Community

The school is itself a community with its own unique identity and spirit. Results of research published on the importance of personally identifying with the school indicate that when such identification exists, there is higher academic achievement, a lower drop-out rate and a reduction in school vandalism. These findings are in the realm of common sense. What is not so easily recognized is that tragedies and crises that are not adequately resolved interfere with a student's acceptance of the school identity.

If a tragedy affecting a large group of students is not satisfactorily settled, the entire group will react adversely and the school community will suffer. A traffic accident, for example, which involves the death of several students has a potentially devastating effect on the lives of both students and teachers. Community spirit and cohesiveness are threatened and the real possibility of reactive, secondary crisis exists. However, if an incident like this is handled in a positive manner, the long term effects will create a unified, compassionate and supportive community for your school.

Fulfilling a Legal Responsibility

Searching nationwide, we found no law which requires that a school system provide specific services in the aftermath of a crisis. The absence of a specific law has not, however, prevented a few juries from holding the school system responsible when a critical incident has occurred. Precedents have already been set in the courts of Indiana and Connecticut where the school was held liable for the death of a student and compensation was paid to the family.

In an effort to protect the school, every crisis must be evaluated for possible liability. If in doubt, check immediately with the school system's attorney. It appears that it may be just a matter of time before there will be a legal imperative for every school to possess and be able to implement its own crisis plan.

Through implementation of the plans and procedures in this book and with proper training of your staff, your school will demonstrate its preparedness to protect and help its students in time of crisis.

Reducing the Effects of Traumatic Stress

Traumatic stress is an emotional crisis precipitated by externally-imposed stressors or situations that are unexpected, uncontrollable, and overwhelming. The survivors of a major traumatic event go through three phases (Baldwin, 1978):

Stage 1 They are stunned and cannot react

Stage 2 Their strategies for coping no longer work and break down. (However, opportunity exists for them to develop new strategies and problem-solving mechanisms.)

Stage 3 Major emotional disorganization occurs

These findings show the reasons why a plan is so crucial: a crisis is a situation which is unexpected and uncontrollable. What type of crisis and when it will occur cannot be predicted, but a flexible and previously worked-out plan will provide the forethought that is not possible during an unexpected event.

Coping Mechanisms Break Down

A crisis situation is emotionally overwhelming. This means that the familiar coping mechanisms of many students and staff will break down (the second stage of crisis reaction) and a disorganization will begin to occur. The timeliness of providing support for the students is critical. If the students are not helped to discover a balanced resolution, they are left vulnerable to disorganization and possible developmental problems.

This organization can be manifested by impulsive behavior, excessive depression, a possible psychotic break and anger toward the school for not adequately addressing the situation. If enough students and faculty are affected, the entire school community itself is in danger of disorganization. (Erickson, 1963)

One Incident of Unresolved Trauma

One junior high school experienced the death of a student who was on the periphery of the student body. Because he was relatively unknown, the school chose not to do anything to acknowledge his death. The teachers were forbidden to hold discussions with the students or comment about the incident.

Junior high schools probably have the greatest grapevine in the world, and within hours of the incident, all the students knew. They tried to whisper among themselves and contain their reactions in the classes but this proved to be beyond their ability because of their impulsive age.

For days afterward, many students were in fights. Others cried with friends and were disciplined for not being where they should have been. Some started skipping school. Three days later, the school psychologists were called to work with the students. By this time, however, the anger of the grief process had been targeted toward the school, its teachers, and principal. Many teachers also were ambivalent about ignoring the death and, through their anxiety, inadvertently communicated their own discomfort to the students. Although the psychologists did work in this school for quite some time, the school never regained the allegiance and the trust of the students.

A trauma shatters the foundations of trust and order expected from authority. Students assume the school is a safe environment composed of people who care about them. When so many distraught students are obviously being ignored, their trust in the world is even further undermined. The erratic behavior and emotional displays are difficult to contain. The school loses control at a time when students need strong control coupled with deep understanding and compassion.

Opportunity Exists in Crisis

In a situation like this, the opportunity of crisis presents itself. It becomes possible for the school to bring students together, forming a sense of community that only comes from a deep sharing. It is not possible for a school to realize this benefit by "taking a business as usual" approach to such an event. Since it is difficult to make all the decisions necessary to contain the crisis and channel the emotional reactions on the day of an event, preplanning will be your greatest asset.

Principals and guidance counselors report repeatedly how invaluable their pre-established plan proved to be during the debriefing after an incident. One thirteen-year-old student said of her inner-city school after a tragedy, "I didn't know they cared so much. They didn't just throw life away!"

Many schools have faced such crises and have responded in ways they felt were helpful but seldom has any sharing of information or formal evaluation occurred. The literature is replete with anecdotal information on how a particular school handled a specific event and, although these articles encourage thinking about preparation, they are not broad enough to indicate guidelines for a plan of action.

It is evident that a mechanism is needed to help many children through the difficult resolution stage. The well-being of the individual student is thereby assured and a healthy strengthening of the collective school spirit occurs as well.

ESTABLISHING YOUR SCHOOL CRISIS TEAM

The reason a crisis *is* a crisis is that by its very nature its occurrence is out of the ordinary and will present unforeseen problems. An in-house crisis team is needed to assess and update continuously its crisis plan. This "quality control" approach will ensure the effectiveness of the plan when a crisis strikes.

The recommendations appearing in this book are guidelines to assist you in addressing the issues arising during a crisis. Not every recommendation will apply to every school or every tragic event. At the end of this chapter is a checklist which can be duplicated, used and reworded by your crisis committee before and after any incidents. Ideally, these guidelines will evolve over time, incorporating changes needed to fit your school.

The Principal's Role

A workable crisis plan must be comprehensive and the task of creating one is a responsibility of the principal which cannot be delegated to anyone else. In the eyes of the community, the principal is in charge of the school. Many decisions that are made in response to a tragedy cannot be delegated. The principal is the one person the community holds responsible for action taken and *not* taken. However, this does not mean the principal operates in isolation in developing or implementing a crisis plan or a crisis team. Every school has many professionals on its staff possessing expertise in various fields. Selecting key people from the staff to serve on an in-house crisis team ensures that all aspects of school life will be addressed. Furthermore, any plan developed by this team should be reviewed by the superintendent's office.

This approach also provides the entire staff an opportunity to air any feelings or fears they might have about how they should handle a crisis. Once secure in their understanding, they will generate the support needed to implement the plan fully. More important, this airing should take place before any actual crisis, thus ensuring that the entire staff will be ready with a definite and positive plan of action when a crisis does occur.

Who Should Be Included?

Just as a President's strength lies in his selection of advisors and cabinet members, the strength of a school crisis plan lies in the selection of the members of the crisis team. The best teams are composed of people possessing the following qualities:

- A broad perspective on life
- An ability to project multiple consequences
- A willingness to challenge an idea and then work cooperatively toward a solution
- An ability to think clearly under stress
- Flexibility
- A familiarity with the nuances of your school, its student body and its community

Members must also be people who are in charge of various school functions and who will bring to the team those specific areas of expertise. Therefore, the team should include:

The principal—This person is the highest level executive in the school and carries responsibility for all decisions made and actions taken.

The principal's assistant or designee—Usually the person who substitutes for the principal when he or she is absent. This person must be someone who commands the same respect and authority as the principal. This person should also be someone the principal trusts to make decisions similar to his or her own way of thinking. Should a crisis occur during the principal's absence, this person must assume and set up a plan with which the principal can comfortably continue.

A guidance counselor assigned to your school. This person should be trained in children's reactions to crisis, emotional stages of grief and group dynamics. Part 3 provides much of this information.

A faculty member—This person should have the respect of co-workers and students alike and be a teacher who knows the climate of your school and is comfortable talking about death.

A security officer—Smaller schools may not have a need for a security officer and you may want to include a local policeman. If one is assigned to your school, he should be on the crisis team. Should the crisis involve an act of violence, your first response must be to provide for the safety of everyone in the building. A security officer or local policeman familiar with the school campus can provide vital information which can help to protect the students and the staff.

A school psychologist—or a member of the district level crisis team will provide information to your team when establishing a plan. The psychologist must also become familiar with the format of your plan should his or her assistance be needed during a crisis.

A school nurse—can provide information and expertise about the physical symptoms of shock or hyperventilation. The nurse can also be instrumental in recommending the logistics for the care and removal of injured students to area hospitals should a crisis require medical intervention.

Functions of the In-House Crisis Team

The in-house crisis team has several functions which are divided into three time frames: pre-crisis, crisis and post-crisis. Prior to a crisis, this team is expected to:

DEVELOP THE PLAN before any incidents occur and gather information necessary to stay abreast of new knowledge about crisis control.

PREPARE THE STAFF for what to expect and train or provide training for them to fulfill their designated roles.

INFORM OFF-CAMPUS RESOURCES about your crisis plan and their possible involvement:

- submit plan to the local school board office for approval, if necessary.
- inform student services department so it can respond when needed.
- inform local police, fire and rescue departments so they know of your preparations.

DEVELOP A MECHANISM through which all crisis team members can be gathered together at a moment's notice in the event of a disaster, to implement the plan.

PERIODICALLY REVIEW THE PLAN especially if major changes have occurred in the school: an increase in attendance; the addition of portable or new structures; new after-school programs; multi-handicapped programs; or an increase in team travel. The plan must also be updated to accommodate changes in the community. If crime in your neighborhood has increased, your plan must provide for any repercussions that might result.

THE IN-HOUSE CRISIS TEAM

Preferred Personality Characteristics:

- a broad perspective on life
- an ability to anticipate multiple consequences
- a willingness to challenge an idea and then work cooperatively toward a solution
- an ability to think clearly under stress
- flexibility
- familiarity with nuances of the school, its students and its community

Staff Members to Have on the In-House Team:

- Principal
- Principal's Assistant
- Guidance counselor
- Faculty member
- Security officer
- School psychologist
- School nurse

Functions of the In-House Crisis Team:

- Develop your school crisis plan
- Prepare school staff
- Inform off-campus resources
- Implement plan during a crisis
- Review plan periodically

ESTABLISHING A SYSTEM-WIDE CRISIS TEAM

Many larger school systems which can easily support a full-time team staffed with well-trained professionals are beginning to establish such system-wide crisis teams to respond wherever crises may occur within the entire school system. This, however, *does not* eliminate the need for an in-house team for your own school. The fact remains that most school districts in America are not large and frequently do not have sufficient funding for such professional teams. These systems build their crisis teams from staff members who hold other positions: guidance counselors, school psychologists, health education teachers and administrators. When a crisis occurs, substitutes are provided to allow these staff members the time to respond to the crisis in their own and neighboring schools.

A Major Issue: Availability

In establishing your system-wide crisis team, answering the following questions will provide you with guidelines for defining its duties:

- Would these personnel be available for just one or two days or could the school depend on them for the lengthy, in-depth follow-up?
- Realistically, how soon could the personnel on the crisis team respond to a call?
- Who would be in a position to drop everything and respond in minutes? in hours?
- Are there others to share the workload but who would not respond until the next day?
- When members of your crisis team are involved in one school for important scheduled activities, such as testing, are they in a position to postpone any activity in case of a crisis?
- To whose directives will the crisis team respond in an emergency?
- What preliminary permissions need to be obtained for the crisis team member to be released from his or her routine duties?

How One School System Does It

The Duval County Schools in Florida have a school-board-based crisis response team, which in its first year of existence was composed of two school psychologists and a social worker. The Supervisor of School Psychology for the system, Pat Howard, developed the team with two goals in mind: first, simply to provide more people who could help a school during a crisis; and, second, to enable the regular school staff to work more effectively by providing them with education beforehand and support and advice during an actual crisis.

Duval County's plan spans three levels:

The Student Level

Ongoing traditional counseling services for students are the bedrock of the Duval County plan. Guidance counselors are trained to help students with grief issues in their lives: death of a parent, divorce, geographic moves, illness in the family. Because this program offers support in individual cases, the mechanism is already there to offer support in a school-wide crisis.

The School Level

Each school has a preplanned system in place for dealing with more widespread tragedies. Everyone has a role to play and everyone knows his or her role in bringing the school back into balance.

The System Level

The school system offers support to individual schools in establishing basic board policies and procedures, providing security systems, dealing with the media, and coordinating community support people. The board's crisis intervention team provides education in crisis prevention, individual counseling and intervention for students, and general support. It also informs the schools about new developments through its contacts with other school districts.

Individual schools can call on the county's team for training at any time. During a crisis, they may call for support, or they may refuse the team's assistance. Others may call on the team as a back-up and appreciate having them there even if they have the situation under control.

ASSESSING THE TEAM'S PREPAREDNESS

Crisis team members must be trained in crisis intervention (much of the necessary information is included throughout this book). It is, however, the actual experience of helping children through grief in their individual lives that provides the confidence and comfort needed to reduce the anxiety and hysteria in some crises. Members must also be comfortable talking about suicide and confronting a student about suicide. They need to be well-versed with the plan in their own school and have a familiarity with the plan of other schools they may be expected to help. They must also be familiar with the strategies for preventing Post Traumatic Stress Disorder (covered in Part III). Finally, a continuous updating of skills is essential for your team. The questions that need to be answered are:

- Where do members lack training?
- How will this training be provided?
- Will the crisis team encompass all situations including violence, death, natural disasters, and bus accidents?

COMPONENTS OF A GOOD PLAN

In developing your plan, there are certain components that must be considered. These are:

1. Gathering the team together.
2. Checking the facts.
3. Adapting the plan to fit the current crisis.
4. Announcing the event.
5. Delineating staff roles and responsibilities:
   - Administrators
   - Guidance counselors
   - Teachers
   - Handling the media
   - Memorial service
   - Parents and the school community
   - The aftermath of crisis

One of the surest ways to guarantee you will follow through on all these components is to develop a checklist for your plan that is readily available to crisis team members. The next few pages contain such a sample checklist to fit this model. When meeting with your crisis team, complete the checklist to fit the logistics and population of your school. Discuss various scenarios with your team as you work. Emphasize specifics such as room numbers, phone numbers, and job descriptions. Focus on details and alternative options. Time well spent at this stage will ensure that clear decisions will be implemented and that you will be in a proactive position when a crisis occurs.

We recommend that your final version be put into a pamphlet for easy access to crucial information. This pamphlet should include names and phone numbers and be kept current. Use the "CRISIS RESOURCE LIST" to keep a complete list of available resources. It follows the "CRISIS MANAGEMENT CHECKLIST." You should also include a floor plan of your school with the location of staff and students for each period of the day. (This is discussed in more detail in Part V, "Coping with a Violent Crisis.")

CRISIS MANAGEMENT CHECKLIST

1. GATHERING CRISIS TEAM TOGETHER

Crisis team members: Phone number   Alternate phone number

_____

_____

_____

_____

_____

_____

_____

_____

2. CHECKING THE FACTS OF THE CRISIS

Some necessary phone numbers:

Police contact person: _____

Rescue squad covering your district _____

Fire department contact person _____

School board contact person _____

3. ADAPTING THE PLAN TO FIT THE CRISIS

Review the following procedures to accommodate current incident. Make a copy of the announcement and faculty responsibilities to give to the staff.

© 1992 by The Center for Applied Research in Education

4. ANNOUNCING THE EVENT TO THE SCHOOL

How will you tell the staff?

Place _____

Time _____

Method of Contact (include telephone tree)

_____

Person presiding _____

Who on staff should be told?

Teachers _____   Bus drivers _____

Guidance counselors _____   Cafeteria Workers _____

Assistants & interns _____   Maintenance Workers _____

Secretarial staff _____

How will you announce the event to students?

Method of contact _____

_____

_____

Person(s) announcing _____

Place _____

Time _____

Written announcement:

_____

_____

_____

5. FACULTY RESPONSIBILITIES

Check off what you want the faculty to do during the crisis.

- ☐ Announce event in classroom
- ☐ Identify students in need of counseling
- ☐ Notify Guidance Office of number of students wanting counseling services
- ☐ Remove very distraught students from the class by having them escorted to Guidance
- ☐ Discuss the crisis (list of suggestions is included in Part I)
- ☐ Postpone testing
- ☐ Involve class in constructive activities relating to the event (list of suggestions included in Part II)
- ☐ Eliminate, shorten and structure assignments for a few days.
- ☐ Discuss with and prepare students for funeral attendance

6. GUIDANCE OFFICE RESPONSIBILITIES

- ☐ Reschedule the following activities

_____

_____

_____

- ☐ Identify individuals who can work with students

name _____ phone # _____

name _____ phone # _____

name _____ phone # _____

name _____ phone # _____

- ☐ Inform feeder schools and area schools so they can provide support for students affected in their schools.
- ☐ Maintain a list of students counseled
- ☐ Call parents of students counseled to provide continued support for the students who are very distressed
- ☐ Select and inform those students who should participate in the Memorial Service in either an active or advisory capacity.

7. ADMINISTRATOR RESPONSIBILITIES

☐ Assign extra secretarial help to Guidance Office

_____ (person & phone)

☐ Contact district personnel for support

name _____ phone # _____

name _____ phone # _____

name _____ phone # _____

☐ Stop notifications on student activity (scholarship reports, testing, placement, attendance) from being sent to the home of a family whose child has died.

☐ Remove personal items from desks and lockers to save for parents.

☐ Rearrange seating, classes, programs, etc. as indicated by crisis. Changes

to be made _____

_____

_____

_____

_____

☐ Establish areas and locations for counseling: assign locations:

name _____ location _____

name _____ location _____

name _____ location _____

name _____ location _____

☐ Keep staff updated

☐ Identify faculty and staff in need of counseling

☐ Emphasize facts and squelch rumors

☐ Remain highly visible

☐ Arrange for excused absences and transportation for students attending off-premises funeral

Crisis Management Checklist, *continued*

☐ Arrange for staff debriefing

Where _____

When _____

Who will preside? _____

☐ Contact parents of students who have died _____

_____

8. HANDLING THE MEDIA

☐ Spokesperson appointed _____

☐ Alternate appointed _____

☐ School board contact person _____

☐ People to handle the telephone _____

_____

Message to be given over the telephone _____

_____

_____

☐ News Release developed

☐ Establish time and location to meet media _____

_____

_____

☐ Identify person to speak to concerned parents

_____

_____

9. MEMORIAL SERVICE

Is a memorial service indicated in this crisis? _____

Crisis Management Checklist, *continued*

How many students will be attending? _____

Location? _____

Presiding person _____

Speakers? _____

_____

_____

Coordinator _____

Student involvement (student names and roles) _____

_____

_____

_____

Activities _____

_____

_____

Area for staff and students not wishing to participate _____

_____

Community people who should be invited _____

_____

_____

_____

CRISIS RESOURCE LIST

Develop a list similar to this using the specific resources available in your community.

School Board Office   *Name—telephone*

    Superintendent _____

    Student Services Director _____

    Crisis Team _____

    Security Officer _____

    _____

    _____

School Support Staff

    School psychologist _____

    School social worker _____

    School nurse _____

    School physician _____

    _____

    _____

Community Agencies

    Youth Crisis Center _____

    Mental Health Clinic _____

    Suicide Prevention Center _____

    Hospice _____

Crisis Resource List, *continued*

Police _____

Rescue Squad _____

Victims' Assistance Office _____

Health and Human Services _____

Rape Crisis Center _____

Clergy _____

_____

_____

_____

_____

Parent Volunteers

_____

_____

_____

_____

_____

_____

_____

_____

_____

_____

_____

_____

PART II

THE CRISIS TEAM IN MOTION

ONCE YOUR TEAM is assembled to handle a crisis you need to immediately check the facts and adapt your plan to the specific incident.

CHECKING THE FACTS

Many school systems have developed a liaison with their local police departments to ensure that they are contacted when an incident affecting the school occurs. This can be vital because it allows the school to put its crisis plan into effect promptly.

Two examples: in the morning news of one city newspaper, a story was printed about a murdered child found in a vacant lot next to a school. When the principal arrived, he discovered it was one of his students. He called the police who were hesitant about releasing any information, thus making verification extremely difficult. However, in another situation, when four high school students were killed in an auto accident on a Friday night, the state police notified the principal at his home. This action afforded time for plans to be well formulated by Monday morning.

In the face of serious trauma, rumors run rampant. Establishing a line of communication with the police BEFORE an emergency arises assures that the facts are received and rumors are dispelled, thus alleviating anxiety and uncertainty.

When Information Seeps in Slowly

There are times when information seeps in slowly as in the case of the USS Starke incident. It took three days for the names of all the victims to be released. Mayport Elementary School immediately established a link with the Navy Family Services and agreed that the school would be informed of the casualties after the families were notified. In an effort to reduce fear, the school provided factual information as it was received and identified all other talk as rumor. In a case such as this, one person on the team should be assigned to control the spread of rumors by providing only factual information and designating other information as false. Particularly in a crisis affecting many people, it is essential to provide ongoing, internal reassurance.

ADAPTING THE PLAN TO FIT THE CRISIS

Adapting your previously developed plan to fit the current crisis is a primary task of the crisis committee. To do this better, or to formulate your initial plan, ask the following questions: (A detailed discussion of each question with sample responses will follow.)

How Will the Announcement Be Made?

- Can you tell your faculty first?
- Is this a school-wide crisis?
- Can you announce the event in such a way that it does not become sensationalized?
- Will rumor and speculation result because of the way the announcement is made?
- How do you expect your faculty, your students, and parents to react to the news?
- Who should be notified within your school system? (Superintendent, school psychologist, crisis team)

Will a Memorial Service Be Held?

- How widespread is the effect of this tragedy on your students?
- Is this an incident that should be memorialized?
- Will the service be open to the public, the press, or parents?
- Set the date, time, and location of the Memorial Service.

Does Your School Have Any Legal Responsibilities in This Incident?

- How will you inform parents?
- What supports, if any, will you provide for parents or the community?

- Are your students or faculty likely to face trials or depositions? If so, how will you prepare them?
- Who can you contact from your school board or community for assistance?

How Will You Address the Media?

- Who is your spokesperson?
- Is this incident likely to draw national attention? If so, who is your back-up spokesperson?
- Has a written statement for the press been prepared?
- Have a time and a location been established to address the media?
- Do you need assistance from your Superintendent's office?

How Much Faculty Support Is Necessary?

- Is it necessary to provide counseling for faculty as well?
- Who will provide this faculty support?
- Have a time and location been established to meet with the faculty after the school day?

When the crisis is over, review and update your school's plan to accommodate necessary changes as they occur. You will most likely need to modify your crisis plan on a regular basis because of changes in your school's makeup. For example, new facilities added to the premises and the growth of the student populace will alter the effectiveness of an existing plan. The addition of a handicapped children's program will certainly increase the responsibility of the staff involved in a crisis plan. Any such changes in the school's character need to be assessed to determine if the present crisis plan remains appropriate.

MAKING THE ANNOUNCEMENT

How the tragedy is announced sets the tone for addressing the loss. The announcement must convey the facts of the incident in a sensitive and compassionate manner. Keeping in mind the shock and the fight-or-flight responses to trauma, you should make the announcement in a way that will contain this intense emotional reaction. (Three samples are provided.)

SAMPLE ANNOUNCEMENTS

In classroom (individual child's loss):

Johnny will not be in school today. His mother was killed in an automobile crash last night. Her car was struck by a truck on Highway 10. Johnny will be very sad for a long time. Perhaps we can discuss some ways Johnny might be feeling and how we can all help him.

In classroom (school-wide loss):

We have something very sad to tell you today. Jennifer was driving home in the rain last night. Her car swerved into an oncoming lane, was struck by another car and went off the road. Jennifer died in the crash. It was sudden and she did not suffer.

Over P.A. system (school-wide loss):

Our school has suffered a great, great loss. Mrs. Doe, the science teacher, has been ill with cancer for many months now. We just received word that her suffering has come to an end and Mrs. Doe has died. We will be commemorating Mrs. Doe's contribution to our school community. At this time, I'd like each class to discuss the ways they would like to commemorate the life work of Mrs. Doe.

Announcement to Faculty

Announcing a tragedy over the PA system places the faculty in a very vulnerable position, since they hear the news at the same time as the students. There is no way of knowing how each faculty member will react to the news, and if a teacher takes longer than the students to move from the shock stage, the students will begin reacting to their fight-or-flight response before the teacher can do anything to contain it. Although most teachers will be able to control their emotional reaction, they are still in an awkward position. They are themselves emotionally strained but need to take charge quickly of a number of students who may soon be out of control. Without a prepared plan, they won't know what to do at this point and the possibility of additional problems related to the crisis reaction is almost a certainty.

Faculty notification depends a great deal on when the news of the event breaks. If possible, sensitive information should be delivered in person. Establishing a telephone tree where each staff member has three names to call provides a pre-established avenue of communication. When time allows, this method can be used to arrange a meeting before school. The faculty can

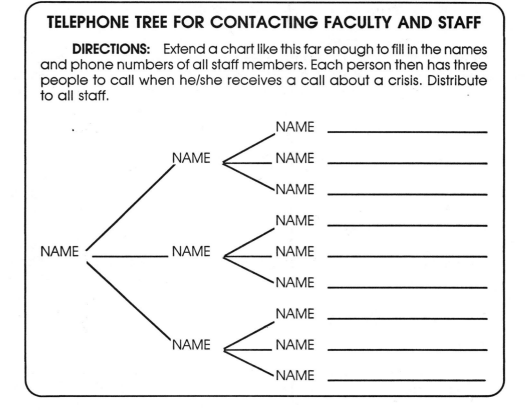

TELEPHONE TREE FOR CONTACTING FACULTY AND STAFF

DIRECTIONS: Extend a chart like this far enough to fill in the names and phone numbers of all staff members. Each person then has three people to call when he/she receives a call about a crisis. Distribute to all staff.

then be personally informed of the tragedy when they are together at the staff meeting. This approach provides the greatest support and it most effectively reduces rumors. However, if time does not allow, the information can be given directly to the staff through the telephone tree. If the crisis occurs during the instructional day, the principal may consider gathering department heads in his office and sending them back to tell their coworkers. In an elementary school, aides can be sent to monitor the classes while the principal speaks to the teachers individually.

Telling the staff first, helps you to maintain maximum control over the school's reaction because the information given is accurate and consistent. The teachers will also have an opportunity to release some of their own grief and offer comfort to each other. Teachers did not choose education as a career to deal with these issues and they will need some reassurance that they are capable of handling the students. The handout "Suggestions for Classroom Activities," can be reproduced and given to the faculty when you review with them the faculty responsibilities. During this review, discuss how to make the announcement to the students This will keep the message uniform. This meeting also offers an opportunity to assess which teachers may be too distraught or uncomfortable to maintain control of the class during the initial reactions of the students. Provide a counselor or another faculty member to help those teachers. If you had planned special annual activities for that day, such as SAT testing, alert the faculty about the need to reschedule.

In one small town, an eighth grade student was killed on a weekend. Most of the students and many faculty members knew of the death before school on Monday. However, one teacher had not heard the news and when he tried to quiet his students and begin class, one student screamed, "I won't sit down, Mike is dead!" The student was 15 years old, still in the seventh grade, and had the reputation of a troublemaker. The teacher did not believe him and told him to sit down. The boy became enraged, turned over a desk and ripped papers off the bulletin board on his way out the door. This situation could have been avoided by using a crisis plan that ensured notification of all faculty members. Fortunately, the guidance counselor worked with the student and helped him direct his anger by using his musical talent to compose a song for the memorial service.

Faculty Defusing

It is crucial to schedule another meeting for the faculty at the end of the day, after the students have left, in order to discuss the day's happenings. Giving support to so many children for an entire day is very draining. Teachers also create emotional bonds with their students and are thereby affected by the loss. Allow them time to discuss ways they might recover from the crisis before facing the students again the following day. Have the guidance counselor or school psychologist brief the teachers on what to expect of the students during the next few weeks and explain how the teachers can help. The support you provide for your staff at this time will enhance the growth of cohesiveness in the student body as well.

STAFF ROLES AND RESPONSIBILITIES DURING A CRISIS

The in-house crisis team should inform the entire staff about its role during a crisis. This action alone reduces much of the anxiety and instills in the faculty and counselors the confidence needed to quiet the students. Discussing staff roles prior to a crisis allows time for expression of dissension and helps to guarantee that the follow-through you and your team have decided upon will take place during an actual crisis. When a crisis does strike and

SUGGESTIONS FOR CLASSROOM ACTIVITIES AFTER A LOSS

- Writing a eulogy
- Designing a yearbook page commemorating the deceased
- Honoring the deceased by collecting memorabilia for the trophy cabinet
- Writing stories about the victim or the incident
- Drawing pictures of the incident
- Debating controversial issues
- Investigating laws governing similar incidents
- Creating a sculpture
- Creating a class banner *in memoriam*
- Building a fitness course, a sign for the school, or a bulletin board in memory.
- Discussing ways to cope with traumatic situations
- Discussing the stages of grief
- Conducting a mock trial if laws were broken
- Starting a new school activity such as a SADD unit if a child was killed by a drunk driver
- Encouraging students to keep a journal of events and of their reactions, especially in an ongoing situation
- Placing a collection box in the class for notes to the family
- Urging students to write the things they wish they could have said to the deceased
- Practicing and composing a song in memory of the deceased
- Discussing alternatives for coping with depression, if suicide is involved
- Analyzing why people take drugs and suggesting ways to help abusers, if substance abuse related
- Writing a reaction paper
- Writing a "where I was when it happened" report
- Discussing historical precedents about issues related to crisis
- Reading to the class (bibliography in the appendix)
- Encouraging mutual support
- Discussing and preparing children for funeral (what to expect, people's reactions, what to do, what to say)
- Directing energy to creative pursuits, physical exercise, or verbal expression when anger arises
- Creating a class story relevant to the issue

the announcement is made to the faculty, it is helpful to review these recommendations and perhaps distribute copies to which the teachers can refer.

The Principal's Role

The authority of the principal cannot be delegated. He/she must be a visible, strong spokesperson, fully involved in the school's recovery, setting the tone and direction for management of the crisis. The principal must:

- Remain highly visible
- Address the media
- Remain in contact with the school board
- Contact the parents of the deceased students
- Address parents when warranted

Remain Visible

It must be emphasized that during a crisis the visibility of the principal throughout the school is crucial to creating order. The students require the presence of authority figures offering support and direction to help them contain their own emotions. The principal, the dean, the vice-principal and any others who are not teaching or counseling should circulate through the halls, the classrooms and the common areas. During a crisis the school should provide firm, compassionate direction through the noticeable presence of authority.

Address the Media

When a tragedy strikes, all eyes are on the principal and addressing the media thus becomes one of his/her most important functions. A spokesperson is often used to handle much of the information going out of the school and that which is disseminated internally. However, when the press is addressed, it is the principal who must release the statement and answer the questions. More detailed information will be given later in this section.

Stay In Contact with School Board

The superintendent entrusts the on-site management of the school to the principal. The perspective and the opinions of the principal are what the school board wants and needs to hear. It is also the principal who possesses the authority to implement its suggestions.

Contact the Parents Affected

One of the major responsibilities of the principal, outside of the school, is to contact the family of the student involved in a tragedy. Because school is such a central part of a child's life, the importance of a visit to the family by the principal cannot be underestimated. A visit makes a connection with the child and brings tremendous comfort to the parents. It is also important for the principal to learn the family's wishes, especially if the cause of death is sensitive, as in the case of a suicide. Many families request the presence of students at their child's funeral. This is healthy for both the parents and the students. The principal should know what kind of accommodations the facility housing the service will have so that transportation of the students can be planned.

Address All the Parents

There are certain conditions which necessitate contacting and addressing parents as a group: when a tragedy occurs on school grounds, when the possibility exists that the school may be held legally liable, or when large numbers of children are traumatized to the extent that the parents are concerned. Addressing the parents then becomes imperative and is crucial for restoring confidence in the school.

The parents' confidence will be bolstered through the involvement of community agencies at the meeting. If the incident involved a security issue, such as a student with a gun on the premises, the sheriff's department might send a representative to discuss restoring safety to the school. If the incident was drug-related, a rehabilitation counselor could discuss the use and abuse of drugs in the community, the signs of drug abuse and how parents can help. If criminal activity was involved and children will be expected to testify, both the parents and the children need preparation which can be supplied by the district attorney's office. Use this meeting or series of meetings to display the commitment the school has to rectifying the problem and helping the children to recover.

Consider the parents one of your greatest resources. Invite them to suggest activities and accept the assistance they may offer. If the influx of calls from parents becomes too much for your staff to handle on the day of a crisis, appoint a parent contact person from your school's PTO.

When the United States Destroyer, the *USS Starke*, was attacked in the Persian Gulf, the media, in its search for information, waited on remote street corners trying to interview children as they left Mayport Elementary School (Florida). The principal used the neighborhood parents to call the school when they observed a media truck heading toward the campus. PTO members were enlisted to stand on street corners before and after school to steer the children away from the press. The parents became a dependable source of assistance during this time.

Even in the event of a less dramatic crisis, it is often helpful for parents to know what type of behavior to expect from their children. It may be helpful to call a meeting and have the guidance counselor and school psychologist discuss with the parents the possible reactions of the children In this way, they can prepare the parents to help avert dysfunctional behavior in the classroom and at home.

The Counselor's Role

The guidance department provides the backbone of a crisis plan. The individual counselors will be the primary persons responsible for alleviating or eliminating potential emotional distress among the students, faculty and possibly the parents. It is critical to the success of your crisis plan that the guidance department is well prepared for the task.

In most crisis situations there is a high demand for counseling services. Planning the logistics to satisfy this demand is a difficult task during the crisis. Finding space for counseling is often a major problem.

Calling On Outside Resources

In developing your plan, anticipate the number of counselors you can expect to be available. Include your own staff, district-level personnel, and counselors from the community. Know beforehand how to contact them and be aware of who is more proficient as group leader or as individual counselor. This can be determined by asking each where he or she feels most comfortable.

Logistics of Counseling

Designate several small private rooms for individual counseling sessions and assign the more experienced and better trained counselors to work with the most severely distressed students. Students less affected are best seen in groups. These groups can be as large as fifteen participants, since the students, individually and as a group, are intensely focused on the crisis. Because the discussion concerns an event all the students share, a room with privacy is not critical. The media center or different corners of the library and cafeteria could easily be used. If weather permits, you may consider conducting a group outdoors.

Some teachers may want a counselor to see *all* their students at one time. If this should occur, it must be emphasized that it is the guidance counselor who determines how the children can best be helped. In some cases, the classes might be too large for a class-group session to be therapeutic. There may also be students who need to be seen individually and for whom a group session could be detrimental.

In one school, an unannounced, well-intentioned teacher converged on the guidance department with her entire class of twenty-five students. The counselor tried to accommodate, but the group session was not effective. Many were too shy to speak in a large group that was dominated by a few students. Some, uncomfortable with their own feelings about the crisis and the large group, joked about the incident and inhibited the free expression of the grief others felt. Both these types of students needed to confront their grief without a large audience.

Coordination By Guidance Office

It is imperative that counseling activities be coordinated by the Guidance Office. Teachers should tally the number of students from their class or home-room requesting counseling and inform the Guidance Department which then schedules the time and location for the sessions and reports this information to the teachers. The count of students must be made twice. The first time is when the tragedy is announced. The second count occurs several hours later because many students may be slow to react, thinking they can handle their emotions. They may find later they really need to talk. Other students might take a "wait and see" approach allowing the first group to report on its counseling experience before utilizing the service for themselves.

If possible, several calls seeking additional counseling support should be made before the onrush of distressed students. The Student Services or Guidance Services Departments of your school board should be notified and requested to redirect the activities of experienced personnel. Usually your school psychologist and school social worker will also provide assistance. You may consider making prior arrangements with proximate schools to share counselors in time of crisis. Any feeder schools could also provide excellent support, since those guidance counselors would already know many of the students.

Other schools indirectly affected by the crisis must also be contacted. Suppose a school bus accident occurs in which several students in a junior high are injured or killed. It is quite possible there are brothers and sisters attending the elementary and high school drawing from the same geographic area. These schools which may, therefore, need to address the crisis issue with their students as well should be informed as soon as possible so they can also determine a plan of action.

Cancel Previously Scheduled Activities

Previously–scheduled activities should be canceled. Even activities such as child-study team meetings, parent conferences and student assessment meetings involving school board personnel must be postponed. Major testing, both psychological and academic, which is usually handled through the Guidance Office, needs to be rescheduled. Not only will the counselor's time be best spent in helping with the crisis, but under the emotional impact of a crisis, the results of any testing could not possibly reflect a true measure of a child's ability or functioning.

Contact Parents

Students exhibiting intense reactions as a result of a crisis should have their parents contacted by the Guidance Department for specific instructions on how they can help their child. Usually there are only a few students so seriously affected and effective assistance can be given through telephone conversations with each parent. When the tragedy seriously distresses a large number of students, it is better to meet with all the parents together after school or in the evening. Reassuring the parents of the school's concern and preparing them for possible reactions will prevent the need for many parent conferences over the next several months.

Get Counseling Practice Regularly

The support of the administration is essential if guidance activities are to flow smoothly. If the guidance personnel spend their time on a day-to-day basis in extraneous, non-counseling activities, they will not be the dependable source of knowledge and strength needed in a crisis. Skills must be practiced if a counselor is to feel confident when handling children in crisis situations. The best way for counselors to develop confidence in their skills before a major school-wide tragedy is by regularly seeing individual children who have had major losses in their lives.

Arrange for Extra Secretarial Support

Your Guidance Department will also need secretarial support during a crisis. If there already is a secretarial staff, provide an additional person for the day. If secretarial services are not included, provide one or two people during a crisis. Knowing schools are frequently understaffed with sufficient support personnel, you may enlist assistance from your PTO. In developing and implementing your plan, identify parent volunteers and train them for specific duties during a crisis. They can then be called upon at a moment's notice and know what to do.

Specific information and counseling activities are presented in Parts III and IV of this book.

Faculty Responsibilities

When a tragedy occurs, the first responsibility a teacher faces is announcing it to the class. She must choose the format best suited to the age level and cohesiveness of the students. Would a group sitting on the floor help to contain the reactions and promote intimacy and support? Would it be better to bring those students who are expected to be especially reactive to a place where they can be assisted more easily without unduly upsetting the other students? Would it feel better having another staff member present while the announcement is made? It often puts a teacher more at ease if she writes or practices with a co-worker, in advance, the message she plans to deliver.

Reactions Teachers Can Expect

Certain reactions can be expected from children in different grades.

A crisis will generally not have a great impact on a child in the primary grades unless the child was very close to the person who died or was present when the incident happened. The issue should be discussed but there is no need to dwell on it. Children this age will, however, react with fear to certain situations, such as someone's parent dying—because the death triggers the fear of their own parents dying. If a child in the class dies of a serious illness such as leukemia, the students must be reassured that leukemia is not contagious. If a violent act has taken the life of a child, the safety and security of the students must be accentuated to reduce their fear of a similar violent act taking their lives. In the case of the child who was found murdered in a neighboring lot, the school followed up with a series of "Officer Friendly" talks on safety.

Junior high and middle school-age children are easily caught up in the sensationalizing of an event. They react with intense exhibitions of emotion or defiant humor to prove how unaffected they are. Students this age are already on an emotional roller coaster and anger will be the predominant emotion. Teachers should expect this as a normal phase of the grief cycle and be prepared with constructive activities to deal with it. The classroom teacher is in an ideal position to prevent a child from entering the disciplinary cycle as a result of this angry reaction to trauma. Seeing the beginning of the anger phase should signal the teacher to direct that student into an activity or a visit to a counselor before disciplinary action becomes necessary.

Although teenagers understand the reality of death, they believe it claims only old people. When this belief is shattered by the death of a student close to their own age, teenagers undergo a real "mortality crisis." It is the teenager's healthy or unhealthy response to this "mortality crisis" which determines, above all, their response to a tragedy. When addressing teenagers about a tragic incident, it is extremely important to discuss the issues centering around mortality: how people bring meaning to life, why death strikes young people, what happens after death, and how people rebuild personal foundations after a tragedy. In this way each young person has an opportunity to begin reconstructing a sense of life's meaning to regain emotional equilibrium.

Class Discussions

Faculty members are encouraged to hold class discussions about a tragic incident when it occurs. The conversation can begin with students sharing memories of the last time they saw the victim alive. This discussion can focus on the good qualities exhibited by the student and on the good times experienced with him/her. It should also emphasize the importance of that student's life and how to cope with the sadness and anger felt from the death. Any student reporting a conflict or a negative situation involving a relationship to the deceased will have a more difficult time coming to terms with the loss. That student should be discreetly encouraged to seek counseling the same day since there may be an experience of guilt that could be devastating. Teachers must also remain alert to any students exhibiting distress or withdrawing into significant silence during the discussion, since they may also need counseling.

Throughout the discussion period the teacher can identify the children who were close to the student involved in the crisis and others who may need counseling. Any students undergoing severe distress should be escorted to counseling by another student or an aide. The teacher, after determining how many other students are interested in counseling, should inform the Guidance Office or the front office and later can direct the students to the correct location and time slot.

Other Traumas Surface

Students often experience emotional upheavals in their lives that the school is unaware of either because the students are wary of sharing the problems with adult teachers or because they may be protecting their families. A crisis can be used to identify and refer these students for counseling follow-up. In their class discussions, the teachers might ask, "How many of you have had deaths in your families? And since many losses feel like a death when they happen, how many of you have had some serious losses, perhaps a divorce, an illness in the family, moving, or changing schools frequently?" By discussing and sharing what helped them most when they had a loss in their lives, children can learn from their own experience how to console each other.

After one such class discussion over the death of a classmate, Mary, a quiet young student in the eighth grade, spoke to her teacher after the class was dismissed. She explained that her parents were divorcing and that her father was not allowed in the home. Since Mary babysat her younger brother after school, she was expected to keep her father out by calling the police. Caught in the middle, Mary was distressed and unable to do well in school. The guidance counselor immediately helped Mary cope with this emotional burden by relieving her of responsibility for her parents' actions. Within a short time, the issue at home was resolved, Mary continued with counseling, and a few weeks later was again doing well in school.

Class Activities

Class time should be used for the students to generate activities and projects that will console the family or commemorate the deceased. Involvement in a positive activity helps direct and contain the emotions. It also provides a mechanism for children to relieve themselves of any guilt and much of the anger induced by the incident.

Because short-term memory and recent learning is impaired when a traumatic event occurs, testing should be suspended for at least a few days. To help release some of the emotions in a productive way, adapt the curriculum to include activities related to the incident. It is not often the opportunity arises to help so many students increase their coping skills, and pertinent classroom activities can be the best source of expanding each student's repertoire of these skills.

English, art and physical education offer natural arenas for such expression. In English, the students can write a eulogy, a memorial passage, or perhaps a story about the student. The art classes can create remembrances in the form of banners, individual drawings, a class drawing, cards and the creation or selection of musical pieces for the memorial service. The construction class can build a memorial, such as a fitness par course in memory of an athlete who died. Civic classes can take on the issue surrounding the incident as a societal problem to solve. Controversial issues can be debated. All of the activities and the many more that can be created by talented teachers will help the students to express themselves emotionally. Resolving any personal conflicts and contributing positively during a time of crisis reduce divisiveness within the school and thereby contribute to a more cohesive school community.

Assignments in the Aftermath of Trauma

In the two weeks following a tragedy, assignments should be more structured and shortened for those students who are especially affected. For instance, if the class is assigned ten problems, a grieving child may not be able to stay on task and finish. The child should be told to write the first problem and then show it to the teacher after it is completed. The remaining nine problems should be assigned in the same manner, one at a time. An older student with a report due can be helped by breaking down the assignment into components. On Tuesday, for example, the books for the report can be selected and approved. In the following week, the outline could be prepared and shown to the teacher. This step-by-step procedure could continue until the student is able to hand in a completed report. In this way the student would not get lost in a myriad of overwhelming emotions.

Handling Personal Grief in Class

In listening to the students on the day of a tragedy, a teacher may also feel tears begin to flow and experience a tightening of the throat. There is no need to hide this reaction. Students can accept the humanity of the faculty and doing so gives them permission to release some of their own emotions without embarrassment. A teacher tells the following story:

> When I was five years old and in kindergarten, my teacher's mother died. The teacher was absent for a few days but we did not know why. When she returned, she explained that her mother had died. She also said that she might be upset now and then but we were told not to worry. In the following weeks there were a few times when tears began to well up in her eyes. When this happened, she would go to the piano and begin to play. We sat around her and sang or listened. All of us felt comforted in the way she handled her grief and could easily understand that she would be sad because her mother died. We loved that teacher and the class was not distressed by her sadness because she was not distressed by it.

THE MEMORIAL SERVICE

A memorial service gives the students the message that life is precious and that each person is of special value. One student remarked after a memorial service, "They didn't just throw his life away. I never knew they (the faculty) cared so much." Choose activities that have continuity, such as planting a tree that will remain for years.

Danny was in the first grade when his teacher died. In the middle of his parents' divorcing, this teacher had provided the nurturing Danny was missing at home. The school children planted a tree as part of their memorial service to her. Even after he was in the third grade, Danny could occasionally be found sitting under that favorite tree thinking "about my problems and

---

STAFF ROLES DURING A CRISIS

Principal:

- Remain highly visible
- Address media
- Contact school board
- Set tone and direction
- Chair crisis team

Counselor:

- Provide counseling for students
- Plan logistics of counseling
- Coordinate all counseling activities
- Communicate with faculty
- Cancel scheduled activities
- Seek additional counseling support
- Contact feeder schools
- Seek additional secretarial support
- Provide information to parents

Faculty:

- Announce events to students
- Lead class discussion
- Identify students in need of counseling
- Generate activities to reduce impact of trauma
- Structure and shorten assignments
- Postpone testing

---

what to do." The school was still providing nurturing for him several years after the death of his teacher.

Who Attends?

The size of the memorial service depends on the popularity of the deceased and the impact the death has had on the student body. When a kindergarten is combined with an elementary school, the death of a fifth grader may have little or no effect on the kindergarten students and they may not need to be included in the memorial service. In high school and junior high school, however, students have broad social spheres and a death frequently affects most of the students in the school.

Where to Hold It

When deciding where to hold the memorial service, determine how large a population must be accommodated. This usually presents a significant problem for large high schools because the student populace exceeds the space available. If weather permits, an outdoor service can alleviate this problem. A facility large enough to accommodate the grieving population should be selected ahead of time by the crisis committee. A space must also be designated for those students and faculty who do not wish to attend.

Who Participates?

One of the ways people resolve grief is by active participation in the commemoration of a death. Involving key students (those who were closest to or in contact with the deceased just prior to death) in the planning of activities and in the actual ceremony, if they are not too distraught, helps bring them a sense of completion. One elementary school used only students in its memorial service. The safety patrol and student council helped the principal plan the service and the students carried it out themselves.

The speakers used at a memorial service might include a trusted counselor, the principal, a clergy member who understands the necessity of a nondenominational service, or a person who had been particularly inspirational to the deceased student. Family members may be in attendance but should not participate in the planning of the program. Their presence should be low-key and they should be seated in an obscure area with an available exit should they become too emotional and need to be escorted out.

Preparing Students

Teachers should prepare the students for the memorial and funeral services. Many young people have never seen a funeral service and discussing one in the classroom reduces any fear they might have. The discussion could focus on the ritual events of the service, how people may react, and what to say while there. This preparation is particularly important to students who are attending the funeral of a student with an ethnic or religious background different from theirs. Unless prepared for it, a child familiar with a very formal religion could be quite upset with a charismatic funeral service; preparation can eliminate that fear.

Debriefing Students

After the memorial service, the students should be brought back to their classrooms to discuss their reactions and feelings. Time should be allowed for comfort and direction to be given. Holding the service at the end of the day and immediately releasing a school full of emotionally charged students could cause problems. Having the students spend time with the teachers and counselors helps bring closure to the incident and prepare the students for their normal routine the next day.

MEMORIAL SERVICE

Sample Programs

I

Procession by safety patrol or color guard
Introduction and opening remarks
Invocation
Message of meaning
Message of appreciation
Closing remarks
Recessional

II

Opening remarks and introduction
Music by choral group or band
Messages of remembrance delivered by 2 or 3 people
Music
Closing remarks

III

Opening remarks
Messages of meaning
Planting a tree/dedication of a memorial
Closing remarks

ADDRESSING THE MEDIA

Principals consistently report that facing the media is the most difficult part of handling a crisis. The responsibility to protect the students and to respond to the community's concern is enormous. This aspect more than any other will require forethought and preparation. Speaking to the press is not a task to delegate. The community sees the principal in charge of the school and responsible for actions taken or avoided. As the visible leader of your school, you must speak to the press and determine the limits of their involvement on your campus.

Building Rapport Before the Crisis

Working with the media actually begins long before a crisis hits your school. Consider the perspective of the newscasters and the community's investment in your school. The citizens have a right to know what is happening in the schools and the reporters see their role as one of bringing important information to the public.

The principal must perform a balancing act, always ensuring that no student is exploited, that the instructional mission of the school is accomplished, and that the community knows how its children's education is being achieved.

This sensitive duty can be carried out best by building an openness and rapport with your local press. Regularly submit information about new programs, successes and awards achieved by your school. When a particular social problem involving children becomes the focus of your local press, offer information and ideas about how you are addressing these issues in your school. Position yourself in the eyes of the media as a resource for information when they choose feature stories related to the children.

For instance, if your local media decide to feature the issue of child abuse, discuss with them the laws governing your staff in the reporting of child abuse. Inform them about programs that you are instituting to train teachers in its detection, and invite them to see the videos or classroom curricula alerting the children to abuse. In this way, the media can see your institution as responsive to the needs and concerns of the community, as having the same deep interest in solving community problems, and, most of all, as being an ally.

When you have won a mutually respectful relationship with your press, you are in a better position to set some guidelines with them prior to a tragedy. It is very important to discuss with your local editors the consequences of covering an adolescent suicide with too much sensationalism (more information is available about this topic in Part V). The Center for Disease Control suggests using its name as a source of the statistics and statements about the media's role in copycat suicides. This sets up an authority outside your school system so that the press cannot misinterpret your actions as uncooperative. Discuss your position and the guidelines you must establish if a tragedy strikes your school.

When a teenage student in a small rural town died of a drug overdose, his parents, needing an outlet for their grief, focused on the school as the target. Although the school had made numerous attempts to help the boy, including encouraging the parents to seek professional counseling, the parents were extremely critical of the school in their statement to the press. Since the principal and the editor had a previously existing professional relationship, the principal was called and given an opportuniy to respond to the allegations. When the editor understood the steps the school had taken, he wrote a factual account favorable to the school.

Limitations of Planning Ahead

What is presented here so far is an idealistic relationship, one you must continuously strive to achieve. Do not anticipate that your efforts will eliminate all the difficulties you may encounter with the media during a tragedy. Most school districts are served by many newspapers, radio and television stations. It is unlikely that you will be able to establish the same understanding with each of them. Sometimes tragedies occur which attract the attention of the national media: the attack on the USS *Starke* in the Persian Gulf; the schoolyard shooting in Stockton, California; and the overturned bus accident in Paducah, Kentucky. Regardless of the rapport you have with the local editor, the person who carries the camera to the site of the crisis is usually a young worker who knows nothing about your guidelines or the consequences of his actions. His sole intent is to get a picture that his editor will run.

Being Prepared for Public Scrutiny

Part of the preliminary preparation necessary involves good management practices. Keep an open pipeline with your staff, students and parents. Encourage people to identify and bring problems to your attention. You cannot be everywhere to experience personally all the events constantly occurring in your school. You must rely on a steady flow of information reaching your desk.

Because institutions are run by imperfect human beings, each has its areas of vulnerability. If you are aware of these areas, you can initiate steps to remedy them. When a crisis occurs, you are then in a position to report your awareness of the problem and the steps already taken or planned to correct it. In this way, you present yourself as knowledgeable and in control of your facility. That is also how you will be perceived by the larger community. The community does not expect perfection, but it does expect you to be correcting your school's problems. Being fully aware of your institution's weaknesses and strengths places you in a more convincing, authoritative position.

During a crisis, part of the preliminary work in addressing the media concerns management practices that will affect your internal public relations. Your leadership sets the direction internally that will be reflected to the public. Providing a strong leadership example with high standards consistently applied will enhance any exposure your institution has to the public. Pride in your community position and your school's reputation will be communicated, diminishing any negative effects from an incident. Operating with candor and respect in all phases of management will heighten your standing within the school and the community. Seeking mechanisms for feedback from constituents will provide you with the insight needed to assess the public's concerns during a crisis. These practices will provide a foundation of strength to sustain your school through an emergency.

When Crisis Strikes

You have a responsibility to keep your staff abreast of information as it filters in. Your staff is an extension of you to the students and possibly to the outside community. They need to be furnished with the facts and the information statement prepared for the community. You must reinforce with them the necessity of squelching rumors. Encourage them to dispel rumors in the classes: find out what different students have heard and then communicate to them the facts that are known; declare all other statements as unknown at the time. It is crucial that the staff be consistent in the facts given.

No one is required to be interviewed by the media. If the media want to interview teachers, you must obtain the teachers' permission and then give your permission. You have a right to deny the press interviews with teachers on the school premises and the teachers have the right to deny an interview at any time or place.

The major responsibility you have as leader of your school is the welfare of the students. Although there will be exceptions, it is best to decline interviews with the students. If it seems appropriate for the student to speak to the press, parental permission must be obtained, preferably in writing. If a more timely response is necessary, parental permission may be obtained by telephone, providing all the calls are well-documented. The decision to allow a student on camera should be very carefully considered, weighing all the consequences.

Alert your internal school support system as soon as word of an incident is received. Depending on the size of your school system, this may include your superintendent or assistant superintendent, your public relations department, the director of student services and the crisis team.

External Public Relations

In all responses, take a proactive rather than a reactive approach. When an incident occurs, you know if it is likely to generate media attention. If you contact the press before they call on you, you establish yourself as cooperative and in control.

Therefore, it is important that you not be the last to know of any incident that occurs outside of normal operational hours. To ensure preparedness, take the time to cultivate a rapport with the police so that if a newsworthy situation arises that affects your school, they will notify you first, at home if necessary.

Johnson & Johnson Corporation faced a most difficult public relations problem when its Tylenol™ product was used as a murder weapon. The plan it developed to defend the company and its products is now recognized as a model for responsibile public relations.

Johnson & Johnson first heard the news through the media broadcast and immediately decided not to avoid the media. They realized their need of the media to reach the public and restore faith in their company and its products. This same approach is needed when a calamity strikes your school. If you view the media as partners through which you carry your message to the community, you will exercise more control over the specific details you want publicized.

Set Limits

You have the right to determine who is allowed on your campus and where they are to be. Use this right proactively by setting limits for the media. In your initial call, inform them as to where, when and for how long you will meet with them.

Establishing geographic and time limits helps you maintain the necessary order needed for reducing distress to the students. To protect the students and the support systems necessary for their well-being, select an interview site outside the mainstream of student activity. A cafeteria, auditorium, or schoolyard, when not in use, can serve this function. The time given to the press need not be more than the time necessary to deliver your prepared statement and to answer a few questions.

Be specific about your requests to address the press: "The principal will address the press in the cafeteria at 10:00 for thirty minutes. A statement will be given, followed by a 15-minute question period. At this time no students or faculty will be available for interviews and no one will be admitted beyond the cafeteria." Reporters in your facility should be accompanied by a staff member familiar with the guidelines you have established.

Prepare a Written Statement

Before the reporters arrive, prepare a written statement with your crisis committee. Since every incident has many facets, there is the opportunity for the story to be told in many different ways. Consistent with your proactive approach, choose the aspect of the incident you wish to emphasize. State the facts and avoid any statement that is speculative. Then tell your story focusing on the positive action the school is taking to help the students. Stress the responsibility the school has assumed by being prepared for a crisis with a pre-established plan. This is also the time to announce any events open to the community: Memorial Service plans (if known at this time), parents' meetings, and follow-up activities for the students.

Your statement should not contain any disclaimers of responsibility until all the facts are known. Your school needs to be recognized as an institution committed to solving the problem and having as its prime interest the well-being of the students. Do not reproach the media for their transgressions. Any attempt to do so creates an image of abdicating responsibility at a time when you need to appear fully in control of your institution.

Your statement must also be shared with your staff. A spokesperson should be appointed to make all the contacts with the media, extending the invitation and informing them of established parameters. The spokesperson should also disseminate this information to the classes, if necessary, and answer incoming calls from the community. Remaining readily available to the public is this person's major responsibility.

The statements you prepare must be truthful. Any falsehood will eventually surface and any attempt to cover up a pertinent fact will come back to haunt you. If you discover you have made an untrue statement, it is better to reverse your statement, suffer the momentary embarrassment, and remain an ally with the public, searching for the truth.

In the Tylenol incident, Johnson & Johnson reported that cyanide, the chemical used in the poisoning, was not used in its factories. When it later learned that cyanide in fact was used, Johnson & Johnson retracted the original statement, although admittedly embarrassed, and presented the facts. The company's candor was welcomed and publicly lauded, thereby increasing its credibility throughout the world.

Once the spokesperson schedules the media interview, it becomes the task of the principal to issue the official statement. Although the school system is governed by a superintendent, the community sees the principal as the per-

SAMPLE STATEMENTS FOR THE MEDIA

"Our third-grade students were on a field trip when their school bus was involved in an accident on I-95. Rescue is on the scene, transporting students to area hospitals. Our vice-principal is also at the scene of the accident now. We have established a special hot-line for parents to call for more information. The number is _____. Our crisis team has gone into action, helping the staff and students. More information will be released as we receive it."

*   *   *

Important points made in this statement are: the preparedness of the school for incidents of this nature; access to information for the parents; responsible immediate action taken by a powerful school representative at the scene; and support already provided for students at the school.

*   *   *

"A fight involving two eleventh-grade students occurred a half block from campus at 7 P.M. last evening. The incident resulted in the fatal shooting of one of our students. Police are investigating and no more is known at this time. Our school's crisis plan went into action immediately following the incident and these are the actions already taken:

- Our crisis committee met last night.
- A parent hot-line has been established; the number is _____.
- Resources have been called in to assist our recovery.
- Counseling for students will be provided.
- Review and reinforcement of our school weapons policy is underway."

*   *   *

Important points made in this statement are: there is no abdication of responsibility even though the incident occurred off campus and after hours; the incident is coupled with a statement about the weapons policy thereby portraying the school as a positive force within the community; access to information is made available immediately for concerned parents thus demonstrating the school's forthrightness; the ability of the school to handle emergencies is proven by its quick response in providing counseling to the students.

son utlimately responsible for the school. Because of this perception, the principal cannot delegate this responsibility to anyone. Even if the school board has a public relations person, the press will still insist upon hearing from the principal.

GUIDELINES FOR HANDLING THE MEDIA

- Develop written statement
- Appoint spokesperson
- Keep staff informed through one person designated to control rumors
- Be proactive with the press
  contact press before they contact you
  set geographic and time limits
  explain restrictions
- Stress positive action taken by the school
- Do not refuse to speak to press
- Do not disclaim responsibility until all facts are known
- Announce new changes made after the incident has passed

Begin to Rectify Problems

When an incident occurs, begin to rectify the situation, regardless of who is to blame. Johnson & Johnson took many steps to remedy its problems. It did not eliminate Tylenol™ from the marketplace, but it repackaged the product. If a serious injury occurred in a school setting during an after-school program, do not eliminate a good program, but do provide for extra safety features to eliminate the cause of the problem. Using the media as an ally, announce the safety changes to the public. You thereby maintain a proactive position of control.

After an incident has passed, it is tempting to avoid public mention of it. If the public believes you or the school share some responsibility for the incident occurring, it is wise to address the media weeks or months later to inform them of new programs or changes you have made. At this conference, it is imperative to thank the media for their interest. Be specific about how you and they have joined together in addressing a serious problem and announce how this joint effort has resulted in changes to carry out further the responsibility the community has placed on you. This will restore the community's confidence in the school. If another incident should then ocur, the community and the media will know from prior experience that you can be trusted to address the problems affecting the students.

Share Responsibility with the Community

Many problems attracting the most media attention are problems of the community and not solely the responsibility of the school. Substance abuse and the crises it creates, namely, automobile accidents and deaths, overdoses and shootings, robberies and beatings, are community problems. The responsibility for these actions must be shared with the community. In addressing the media, the principal can highlight how much the school is doing to alleviate a particular societal plague and should stress the importance of all sectors of the community working together to provide solutions. The spokesperson could also invite other people involved with youth to comment on the issue: the State Attorney's Office, Health Department, Law Enforcement Agency, rehabilitation personnel, religious youth leaders. Adolescent suicide is a prime example of a community problem. It is, therefore, the community's responsibility to address it. Recognize and accept your role as one of the major leaders of the community able to help solve the problems of youth. You will then establish yourself as a prime resource for helping the community without accepting all the blame for its problems.

Communication with Parents

Inform and include the parents of your students when responding to any public attention generated by a crisis. Provide a meeting at which concerned parents can voice their opinions and through which you can enlist their assistance. The most likely source of serious or legal problems which will be compounded by the media are the parents, since they are the people outside your school with the most vested interest in its daily activities and events. Keeping the parents informed about events that have happened builds their trust. By listening to their concerns, you are positioning yourself as their ally. Inviting a recognized community expert to speak on the subject under scrutiny will answer the parents' questions, provide additional support for the school, and share the responsibility with the community in addressing the issue.

An effective use of this approach occurred after a school had a shooting in one of its classrooms. The police were involved in the apprehension and investigation of the individual; the State Attorney's office focused on testimony by the children; and community mental health services helped the children through the emotional trauma caused by the event. During the parents' meeting which the school had convened, speakers were used from each of these resources. Mental health personnel spoke about the emotional and behavioral reactions the parents might anticipate in their children and how they, as parents, could help; police officers addressed the issue of security provisions used by the school and described the safety assurance talks that would be given to the students; the State Attorney's representative explained the legal procedures the children would be facing. The school was recognized for its superb accomplishment in bringing together all the sources of assistance the children, their families, and the school personnel had required.

The Media's Point of View: Two Perspectives

This section on "Addressing the Media" concludes with two interviews. The first is with a television reporter, the second with a television news editor. Their statements are to the point. They do not always agree with each other and they do not necessarily see critical issues from your perspective. Both will help you understand what you will face during a crisis involving media presence. This awareness is critical to all members of a crisis team to ensure that proactive, not reactive, choices and decisions are made when a crisis strikes.

A Television Reporter's Perspective

Following is an interview with Carolyn Broughton, in which she discussed her experiences as a reporter for a CBS television news station:

> You school principals have to be sensitive to the fact that I realize you are trying to organize people and calm the situation there, but I've got thousands of people who want to know what's going on and they can't get through. Your phone lines are busy. If you allow me, I can get some of the information out for you. The news media then can become an arm or extension of your communication. This is one of our objectives.
>
> We want to inform parents. Should they come to the school to collect their child, should they stay home, is there a central point that everyone's been invited to that they should know about? If we'd be given information like that, the school system would not have to contact all the parents. We can help spread the word.
>
> All of these things are more easily facilitated when a healthy relationship exists between a principal and the press prior to a crisis. What I've done to promote that relationship is present a variety of feature stories: school board meetings, interviews with principals and things like that. Perhaps it would help if principals went out of their way to introduce themselves and say, "I'm Principal of such and such a school. I'm glad to meet you." This way a principal knows ahead of time which reporters he trusts

and to whom he would give a story. If they just become more friendly, instead of avoiding the media, they'll get a good feel of whom they can talk to. When you run into reporters who distort what you say, give them minimal information. But at least by meeting the press, you can determine who you will give what information to. But you can only know this if you make an initial contact before the crisis.

It's a reciprocal thing. I had previously been at a high school talking to the students about drinking and driving. When the principal saw me, she suggested I do a human interest story about a student in her school for whom they were trying to raise money to travel to south Florida to receive an award she had won. Neither she nor her family could afford the trip. It was a great story. The principal and I built a fine rapport and I had the good feeling that I had helped this child by something I had done. When a crisis later arose at the school, I called the principal and told her I was just looking for some insight and direction for the story. Because of our previously established relationship, we were able to work together in a nonadversarial way.

When you find a few reporters who are insensitive to the needs of the school and the students, don't exclude them from a story. It will only make the situation worse. When they ask you questions, answer without volunteering information. You can give them different levels of information. If you cut them out, they'll get resentful.

In fact, the term "no comment" is very dangerous, because the public has come to view that as, "Oh, they're hiding something." It's always better to say something other than "no comment." Even in a crisis, if you really don't have information, just say, "I don't know yet, but I will get that to you as soon as possible," or "We are still evaluating it and we'll get back to you." That's better than nothing.

If this is the first contact with that reporter, he may not believe you and may go to other sources to check out what you are not saying. That's why it's important to meet the reporters as soon as possible.

Don't call about every single little story. Wait for what you think may have interest to the entire community or ties into a national theme.

When the media want to talk to students, the principals can assist by choosing the students who they know are most in control, perhaps the student council members. A good principal should approach some of the more controlled students and say, "Look, I think we'll be approached by the media. Do you think you could handle speaking with the press about this situation?" If the principals chose and asked the students ahead of time, it would smooth the way for a story. Then tell the press, "We have some students who have volunteered to share their thoughts with you." Reporters in a hurry will take what they can get and they'll not pass up an offer like this if it's not obviously staged. Don't coach the students. Don't put words in their mouths. It sounds very staged.

The deadline for the evening news is usually four o'clock. This gives ample time for reporters to obtain the parental permission necessary for those students who may appear on TV. A principal can say, "You cannot speak to any students now, but by this afternoon, I will have some to speak with you."

What does the public demand to hear? Well, in the case of a person barging into a school with an AK-47, they want to know how this person got into the school, what security procedures existed, is there any way to prevent this from happening again, what kind of medical facilities are available, how will the teachers respond to the situation. If a roof falls in and hurts a student, they'll want to know about the building's maintenance records.

How can the school get coverage after problem areas previously reported by the media have been corrected? First, find out which reporters had covered the initial story. Talk to them to see if they're interested in the followup. Invite them to a planning session to discuss the problems and how to change them. If they do not want to come, send them the results. Include the thoughts and opinions of parents, teachers, and students. Usually it's a much more interesting story when students are involved.

It is always good to let the press know when any new program will go into effect. Invite them to participate either just before a program starts or the week it begins. Give them a hook—this is a model program, this is the first day of this program—something that's timely or really new.

To establish a working relationship between the media and the schools, it is imperative for the principals or school superintendent to get to know the news editors and the reporters. One time I had a school board member ask if it would be possible to spend a day with me while I was doing a school feature story. That certainly helps to establish rapport. If I know the principal or board members ahead of time, I am less inclined to think that something is being hidden.

There's a lot of pressure on reporters from their editors and the community to sensationalize the news. They want to see the bleeding and the crime. Not everyone, of course, but the pressure is there. Some editors want to show the crying and grief on a person's face. As a reporter, I put myself in that person's place and I wouldn't want that. Knowing I have to get a story, however, I try to approach the person gently, by saying, "I know you are upset and confused right now, but would you mind making a statement you could share with the public?" If the person says no, I respect that.

A Television News Editor's Perspective

The following is from an interview with Michael Crew, News Editor, Channel 17 (ABC), Jacksonville, Florida:

The belief that an adversarial relationship exists between the principals and the media is not entirely unfounded. We approach a school principal as someone who has an obligation to paint the best possible picture of certain elements of a disaster. There may be some culpability on the school's part, a failure in the staff, something structural in the building, something collapsed. It may involve an issue of accountability to the supervisor of the school system. So we assume the principal, and, going on up, the school administration, are a single source of information. We do not consider them the only source.

We will be constantly seeking, using many points of view, to find out what really happened. There's going to be the point of view of the principal, the parents, the children, the teachers, the participants and the bystanders. There is an adversarial relationship in that we won't accept the principal's statement as the only point of view. We're going to do whatever it takes to get what we need. We understand that principals have to try to get their point across but they need to understand that we're going to take that as a point of view and not necessarily as fact. Then they'll be better able to understand what it is that we're going to be doing.

The school organization is not very good at keeping parents informed. Most of our calls involving school situations involve parents who are frustrated because they can't find anything out. Our job is to get out information that people want. That's our first job. Our second job is to get out information about the story that they will probably want. Take the instance in California with the assault rifle; the first thing the parents want to know is, "Is my kid all right?" Accurately reporting on how many children have been injured and what is happening to the children who have not been injured is what's important. We can often be useful in getting out information to the 1,500 or 2,000 parents involved here rather than having all those parents descend on the school. Rarely do school personnel understand that if they dealt with us, they wouldn't have to deal with all those parents—better a handful of reporters than 2,000 parents.

Is there any way that principals can establish a rapport with the media prior to a crisis in order to smooth the time of crisis? I don't know that they can. It's very difficult for a single principal to build a rapport since most of our dealings are with his bosses, the school board. There are hundreds of principals within our coverage area and I don't know half of them. The principals are going to have to realize that part of their responsibility is for them to quickly and accurately disseminate information. The press is going to get information one way or another and we're going to broadcast it. If we're getting hearsay and rumor only, we're going to go on the air saying that's what we're getting and that no more is available. Our assumption is that if they're not telling us something, they're obviously trying to hide something. Let's find out what they're trying to hide. And that's the quickest way to get into an adversarial relationship—by trying to hide something or lying. If they try to lie to us, that's another story in itself. Our assumption is, if they're trying to lie to us, they're trying to lie to the public.

There's one area where I particularly get sore and that's when there's been a serious crisis and counselors are needed to talk to the kids. They won't let us interview the counselors to let us see what it is they do with the kids. How do they help them? What do they do? They've missed the boat in three areas. First, they've failed to get information out to the parents about what's being done to help the kids and how. The parents could possibly learn and use these same techniques. Second, they've kept this information from other schools that eventually might have occasion to use it. And third, they've failed to recognize we are a society that is media-permeated. The media is not going away.

If you watch the news, you'll see a whole lot of peoples' lives that make up the grist for the mill that day. Now, you don't want your life in it but you're perfectly willing to sit there and watch someone else's life. That double standard doesn't exist for us. Kids are also going to be asked some questions by people with cameras and lights. That's reality. Some people it helps, some people it doesn't. We try to be very sensitive in these situations. We would never go up to a kid in a crisis situation and stick a camera in his face. We would always ask first.

We would also be suspicious if a principal lined up certain kids to present to the press. If the kids were told, however, that the press was going to be around a certain part of the campus and that those who didn't mind talking to them could be there, then what they had to say would be more credible. We will go with that, as long as it's left up to the students. What we are looking for are the human elements to communicate to the rest of the world because oftentimes the truth cannot be communicated by facts alone.

For the most part, we don't do suicides. There are no hard and fast rules, however, and each instance has to be judged separately. And there's no "right" decision. I have never walked into a situation where I felt I made the absolutely "right" decision. You have to be careful, too, about the public's right to know. The public has the right not to have information withheld but they don't need to know everything. We're not in the tabloid business. The bottom line is, "Are we putting out useful information? Can you do anything with what we're telling you? Are we essentially advancing anyone's understanding?"

There are four essential points that principals need to realize about the media: first, our society is a media-permeated society and that has to be accepted as part of the plan. Second, the adversarial relationship that exists between the press and the principals is a fact to be accepted because the press believes it represents a large group of people, the parents, who want to see everything done right by the school for their children. Third, the second point being true, be prepared to come under scrutiny as principal. Fourth, understand that the different media have different agendas and even among themselves are in competition. The competition will play a part in how they conduct themselves during the newsgathering.

THE AFTERMATH OF A CRISIS

The time to help students and staff put a crisis event in perspective occurs when the incident is over and emotional and physical exhaustion have set in. Now there will be time for the affected individuals to

- Search for meaning in the event.
- Understand and accept their own emotional reactions; and
- Increase their ability to cope with future adversities.

It is during this healing time that you can

- Promote maturity and growth in the students and the staff.
- Integrate the emotional investment of the students into a loyalty toward their school; and
- Refine your plan.

Debriefing the Faculty

Within the first three days, usually the first, set aside time for the faculty members to have their debriefing. This can be attended voluntarily, and co-facilitated by both the guidance counselor and the principal. Also encourage all the crisis team members to participate.

Teachers should be asked about their reactions to the events of the day and their input for improvement. Discussion should end with ways to take care of oneself with participants encouraged to commit to one nice thing they can arrange for themselves that afternoon or evening.

This meeting usually takes about thirty minutes and gives the important message to the teachers that the administrator also cares about them and values their perspective. The same loyalty generated among the students could also occur among the staff. What manager would ever pass up such an opportunity to endear herself/himself to the employees just by offering timely compassion?

In an evaluation of a crisis plan, two months after the death of two students, many teachers commented on how superbly the school handled the students and wondered why they did nothing for the teachers. Many felt devalued and cheated.

Debriefing the Crisis Team

In the aftermath of a crisis, you must debrief not only the faculty, but also the principal, the Guidance Department, and the rest of the crisis team. Also include anyone else who was integrally involved with the activities of the day. First, reconstruct the actions taken by the team. Since hindsight offers so much insight, you will be able to reevaluate your plan, identifying those actions you did right and those decisions that could have been improved. This will allow you to customize your plan to reflect the needs of your particular school. Experience gained by some staff members will not be lost if they are transferred.

Such evaluation is not the only reason for the debriefing, however. You and your team would have to be of stone not to be emotionally affected by the decisions, the events and the responsibility taken on the day a crisis occurs. Most people in helping positions forestall their reactions in order to fulfill their responsibilities and offer assistance to others. Therefore, the second level of debriefing should be a time for the crisis team to also share its emotional reactions with each other. Although your first instinct may be to just get away and go home, giving yourselves a few minutes to ventilate will insure your emotional readiness for the next crisis, should one occur.

Ongoing Counseling of Students

Most of the work in the aftermath of a crisis will fall upon the shoulders of the guidance counselors. One or two groups (of 6-8 students each) should be formed, inviting anyone who wishes to participate. Students who are particularly at risk due to the crisis should be referred to the group. In some cases when class schedules could not be accommodated, counselors have established a brown bag lunch group that met weekly.

A few students may also require individual sessions if their problems are different from those of the other students or if they are so intensely upset that group participation will also intensify the reactions of the rest of the group. For example, in one incident, a young man of fifteen accidentally shot and killed his best friend while playing with his father's rifle. Although the other students offered understanding and compassion to the boy, his guilt would have been exacerbated by listening to the group's reaction to the death and would have stifled its need to share.

Parts III and IV provide information and activities for guidance counselors, equipping them with the skills necessary to support and guide students and faculty through the aftermath of a crisis.

SUMMARY

You have been provided with the guidelines to develop your own plan. To individualize such a plan for your school, follow the steps outlined to form a crisis team. Then with your team discuss each phase of the crisis plan, making detailed decisions such as which rooms to use, who calls whom, etc. List the team's decisions, circulate among all members for additional "afterthoughts". Revise the plan accordingly. Keep this plan and all supporting forms in a file folder for each crisis team member. You may want to keep a copy at home and at the office. If the crisis is a fire in the school, you may not be able to get to the plan and obviously will not remember every detail.

These are general guidelines only. You and your team know more about your school, staff, students and community than any outsider. Do not hesitate to adopt changes that are more appropriate for your institution. However, throughout this book the rationale for the suggested actions is given; if you change the actions, make certain the rationale justifies your action. Avoiding actions to avoid controversy or dealing with delicate issues has a high potential to backfire making an issue even more explosive than it might have been.

PART III

CRISIS COUNSELING

Introduction

THE HEALTH AND well-being of the students in the aftermath of a crisis will be primarily in the hands of the guidance counselors. Part III gives explicit information about the crisis-reactions you can expect and an understanding of children's perceptions at different developmental ages. Part IV provides a selection of easily accessed activities designed for specific age groups and specific problems.

The information sections in Part III will provide you, the counselor, with the background knowledge to feel confident and competent prior to an event occurring. Then the activities in Part IV can be accessed at a moment's notice and used as the need arises.

EFFECTS OF TRAUMA ON CHILDREN

Disappointments and surprises in our lives bring changes in the way we develop. All the changes, even the seemingly simple ones, carry an emotional toll. Change puts us in unfamiliar territory and, being unsure of ourselves in a new situation, we remain uncomfortable until feelings of competence and security are again established. This adjustment to change will be either positive (healthy) or negative (unhealthy).

A child is often exposed to change: moving from one grade to the next, winning or losing a swim meet, or having a new sibling join the family. The opportunity to learn healthy adjustment to these changes is always present. With any of these changes, however simple they may appear, something is left behind to make room for the new and it is at this point that grief will be felt. We grieve for what we leave behind and for those things that never were what we hoped they would be. These unmet expectations and the ensuing disappointments are fertile experiences for building coping skills.

It is through these life experiences, beginning in our childhood, that we learn to understand, accept and handle our emotional reactions to a crisis. By the time we become adults, we have a strong repertoire of coping skills upon which to rely. But how can our children recover from serious tragedies with only seven, twelve or fifteen years of life experience on which to draw? We must be prepared to guide them along a healing path.

Within the school the entire student body changes after experiencing a tragedy involving one of its own people. If the crisis is handled in a sensitive, compassionate manner, the classes will bond to form a cohesive school community that relies on and respects itself. If the crisis is "tucked under the rug" or only superficially acknowledged, students will have only their own resources on which to rely and they are often inadequate. When the internal resources do not provide the necessary emotional support for a child, his emotions will erupt in maladaptive behavior.

Children can learn compassionate behavior but they need very specific direction in what to say and do. One elementary school suffered the loss of a third-grade student who was not well-liked by her classmates. Many children easily slipped into thinking that she therefore deserved to die and that "God punished her." To counter that belief and to teach that every life has meaning, the school focused on the love she had shown for animals. The children readily acknowledged this kindness to her pets and, in memory of the deceased child, collected pet food for the Humane Society. The students were also given a very powerful message that all life has meaning.

If this incident had been handled less sensitively, many children might have held to the conviction that their classmate's death was a punishment. And if any of the children holding that belief were to experience later the death of someone close, tremendous guilt feelings could easily result. The child could believe, "If I had not been bad, my loved one would not have died." This belief arises from the "magical thinking" that occurs during the middle childhood years.

AGE LEVEL AND PERCEPTIONS OF DEATH

The age of a child and a perception of death must be taken into consideration when developing your crisis plan. The developmental, not the chronological, age of the child is the critical factor. If your school has developmentally impaired children, you must remember that it is their age of understanding, not their chronological age, that determines their reactions to a tragedy. On the other hand, the intellectual understanding of gifted students far exceeds their emotional ability to cope with death.

If a child is chronologically six years old but has a developmental age of nine, he is emotionally six and intellectually nine. A six-year-old child does not have the emotional capacity to cope well with a real knowledge of death's finality and usually does not believe the deceased is gone forever. If this six-year-old is intellectually advanced he will understand the concept of death's finality but will not have the emotional strength to cope. Because of this, he will need direction both in helping to build sufficient coping mechanisms and in finding a sense of meaning in the death.

Preschool and Kindergarten Age Group

A child below the age of five usually has no understanding of the finality of death. The pain of grief is in the separation. Today's children of five have grown up watching Saturday morning cartoons where the characters routinely undergo physical bludgeonings one minute and return unscathed the next. Death and its finality is not a reality.

The five-year-old child who has suffered a traumatic loss will re-experience the grief again at about age eight when the concept of finality is understood. The child then knows the deceased are NEVER coming back. If a class has experienced a major tragedy in those early years, or even a less traumatic loss, it may be helpful to discuss the loss once or twice when this finality is understood. The discussion can be used to validate the earlier experience and identify how different students handled the situation. This approach builds confidence in the students about their ability to cope when serious problems arise.

When Brenda was three years old, she saw her father shoot and kill her mother. Her father went to prison and Brenda went to live with her grandmother in another state. She was treated in therapy for the trauma and for many years functioned very well. Then, in the third grade, she began to have nightmares again and both her grades and behavior in school deteriorated. Brenda was beginning to understand more completely how permanent the death of her mother really was. With counseling she soon regained her equilibrium and continued to do well.

Communicating with the Young Child

It is imperative for adults to be absolutely clear when communicating with a child of this age group. They are extremely concrete in their thinking and the words they hear are taken literally. "Rest in peace" becomes equated with sleep and "eternal rest" sounds boring to a five-year-old child. Clear communication is especially important concerning the events surrounding the funeral and the viewing of the body. Whatever the young child sees and hears is subject to literal interpretation. One young child attending her grandfather's funeral noticed the blanket of flowers across the closed half of the casket and when leaving asked her mother, "Why did they cut Grandpa's legs off?"

Young children also possess a graphic vision of life after death. Life-like needs are attributed to the deceased both in the grave and in the children's concept of heaven. When asked to consider the needs of a person after death, children of this age respond with:

- "The box they are buried in keeps them warm."
- "They are fed in heaven."
- "In heaven you can eat all the ice cream you want and never get sick."
- "In heaven people sleep on clouds because they're so soft."

Six-to Eight-Year Age Group

During the years six to eight, the child is developmentally tackling the concept of living and nonliving things. Anyone who has worked with children of this age is well aware of an almost morbid curiosity about death. This is the age when children will stick a pin in a bug and watch how long it crawls before it drops. After a period of time, one child may exclaim, "He's still dead!" and for that child a great discovery has been made. The themes in their play reveal their preoccupation with life and death. They are earnestly trying to grasp the reality of death and its finality.

Fascination with Ritual and Detail

At this age, ritual is so fascinating that even in the event of a tragedy, the child's interest becomes immersed in all the arrangements. He can be very distraught one minute and in the next, occupy himself with probing questions about what will happen at the funeral and whether worms will eat the body when it is buried. Adults are frequently put off by these seemingly disrespectful remarks.

You may wish to explain this outlook to parents and teachers so they do not inadvertently discourage communication. A child of this age has no reluctance to discuss death or its aftermath but he quickly senses from the adult world the non-verbal signals requesting him to keep quiet. If the adults in that child's world are uncomfortable with the type of questions he asks or if they disregard them as inconsequential, he will stop questioning and be forced to resolve, in isolation, the trauma that the death presents.

Eight- to Twelve-Year Age Group

Until this age, the grief a child feels from a death relates to the separation of the moment: "I miss my mom because she's not with me." The thought has not occurred to the child that he will never see Mom again. The child of eight, however, begins to understand the finality of death. The grief he now feels, in addition to the separation of the moment, is from the pain of knowing death is forever.

Egocentric thinking patterns predominate in this age group and result in "magical thinking." As a result of this self-centered thinking, the child infers he has more control over his world than is humanly possible. He believes that his wishes can come true and that the actions in which he engages CAUSE the events in his life. Adults know that other people react to their behavior, but they also know that their behavior is not the CAUSE of the reaction. A child does not perceive this subtle difference.

A child, for example, will walk on his mother's rug with muddy feet and his mother will get angry and reprimand him. The reprimand is a consequence. The mother had the choice to react in many different ways but chose the anger and reprimand. The mother could have nostalgically remembered such a day in her own childhood and laughed at seeing her son in the same situation. Although the mother had the choice, the child feels he made his mother angry.

Many educators have seen the child whose family is separating. The child creates crisis after crisis because he quickly learns that when he causes enough commotion, his mom and dad talk to each other without fighting. His acting-out serves the function of holding the family together for a brief period. Ultimately this does not work because his behavior, whether good or bad, will not mend the marriage any more than it will create the divorce. In the aftermath, though, the child interprets the sequence of events to mean he has caused the divorce. He believes, "If I wasn't so bad, Mom and Dad would be together."

The same thought pattern appears when a death occurs, especially the death of a sibling. Very few children go through life without occasionally wishing to be the only child in the family. Sibling relationships in middle childhood years are often love-hate relationships. Many children have at one time or other wished a brother or sister dead. If that death becomes a reality, the child feels guilty. Because of his own egocentric thinking, the child believes he caused the death by his wishful thinking. He consequently also feels responsible for the pain his parents are experiencing. It is this sense of responsibility and the guilt it creates that make it imperative these children be given ample opportunity to discuss a death.

Teenage Perception of Death

Abstract thinking begins at age 12. This is the age when the full concept of death is understood. Teenagers understand death on the same level of understanding as adults, but with one difference—they believe people die when they are old and have done everything they want to do with their lives. They operate on the assumption of the immortality of youth.

When a death intrudes on this assumption, he/she goes through a crisis. The crisis is the realization that the young, too, can die. The teenager who has a family or support system with sound values and clear communication, a spiritual or philosophical foundation to draw upon, and the self-esteem generated by some personal achievements, will weather this crisis beautifully. Both strength and sensitivity will develop that will be manifested in any life choices.

A teenager who loses a brother or a sister will frequently focus career goals on solving the problems related to the death. In this way the idealism that is inherent in the teenager's attitude is restored. "An injustice was done, but I will make it right in the world." The youth whose brother died of cancer chooses a career in cancer research, and the teenager whose friend was killed by a drunken driver starts a SADD unit (Students Against Drunk Driving) in her school. These are healthy responses.

The Teenager at Risk

The young people educators must concern themselves with are those who lack a solid emotional foundation. These are the students who express their grief with, "If I can be wiped off the face of the earth tomorrow, why should I study today?" They are at risk for substance abuse, sexual promiscuity, dropping out of school, and suicide. These students have lost their meaning of life through a tragedy that destroyed the assumptions by which they live.

It is especially important to be aware of these students when you face a traumatic death in your school. Usually attention is given to those students who appear to be directly affected by the loss, but it is essential to address all the students because there is no way of knowing which students are undergoing a crisis reaction resulting from a lack of internal support. Teenagers even remotely touched by the death will ask themselves, usually for the first time, "What does it all mean?" In developing your plans, consider ways to reach out to those affected through their own questioning as well as those students affected because of their closeness to the deceased.

Loss and the ensuing grief are cumulative in intensity. If a person suffers many losses in a brief period of time, the resolution is more difficult because of the multiple grief-causing situations. Your students face many

AGE-SPECIFIC REACTIONS TO LOSS

Age 6-10: primary method of expression is play/art/music

- Reduced attention span
- Radical changes in behavior (out of character)
- Fantasizing event with savior at the end
- Mistrust of adults

Age 10-12 in girls, 12-14 in boys: more childlike in attitude

- Anger at unfairness
- Excitement of survival
- Attributes symbolic meaning to events (omens)
- Self-judgmental
- Psychosomatic illness

Age 13-18 in girls, 15-18 in boys: similar to adults

- Judgmental
- Mortality crisis
- Move to adult responsibilities to assume control
- Suspicious and guarded
- Eating and sleeping disorders
- Alcohol and drug abuse
- Loss of impulse control

difficult losses in their young lives: divorcing families, geographic moves, child-shuffling (the child who lives with mother until she feels she cannot cope, is then shuffled off to Grandma and finally to an uncle before the academic year is completed). Each of these moves involves a loss of friends, important adults, and familiar environment. When multiple losses occur, the child has to postpone any emotional reactions to grief in order to cope with an every-day existence in a world already involving numerous changes.

In adjusting to change, the child focuses on learning and refining adaptive behaviors necessary in a new life situation. By focusing on the current adaptation, vey little time is spent on the grieving process and the child begins to deny and suppress any sad or angry feelings. The more adaptation time this child needs, as is the case when many changes occur too quickly, the less time and energy is available to complete the grief cycle.

When a tragedy occurs in a school, it often affects many children who are already coping with multiple losses in their lives and the impact of the tragedy then triggers the reaction for all the other losses. A trained staff can identify children beginning to exhibit disproportionate reactions to a current tragedy and thus prevent them from entering the discipline cycle.

In 1986, Ribault Junior High School of Jacksonville, Florida, provided counseling throughout the day for groups of students coping with the death of an eighth-grader hit by a car. One student in a counseling group refused to speak although she had requested to join the group. Afterwards, she quietly told the counselor that her mother was dying of cancer and the family was moving out of state so that her mother could get treatment. No one in the school knew of her mother's illness or that they would be moving soon. This information provided an opportunity for the school to help the child make the transition more smoothly.

SHORT-TERM REACTIONS TO TRAUMA

When a crisis strikes, people respond with a fairly predictable physical and emotional pattern. The intensity and manifestation of this pattern vary with the individual. The initial physical response is an inability to move, accompanied by an emotional response of disbelief, denial, and numbness. This stage usually ends in a matter of seconds, giving way quickly to the fight-or-flight response. The body prepares for danger: the heart beats faster, adrenalin enters the system, and breathing is accelerated while a cataclysm of emotions erupts—rage, fear, terror, confusion. Finally, the body physically exhausts itself and the mind begins the slow process of emotional restructuring.

The implications of these reactions need to be considered when developing your crisis plan. As the news is announced, the first response (phase one) will be the inability to move. In most instances, the staff will move so quickly out of this phase it may appear as if it did not occur. If, however, in deciding how to announce the event, a classroom teacher takes longer to move beyond this reaction than one of the children, the child could be in his fight-or-flight response before the teacher has regained the composure to handle the situation.

When a tragic event is announced over the PA system, the teacher is placed in the very vulnerable position of having to deal with her own distress and simultaneously provide guidance to her students. There is no way to know, before an event occurs, how a staff will react. Placing them in this dilemma decreases the control over the subsequent sequence of events. After a shooting occurred in a second-grade class, one young student bolted from the classroom, left the school and ran two blocks to his home before the teacher's aide could respond.

Whether the students can control it or not, the fight-or-flight response will be there and young people will need activities through which to ventilate their emotions. Because the children, by themselves, cannot contain their intense emotional reactions, organization of the counseling sessions and related activities is essential to keep reactions manageable. The reactions will include crying, running away, fighting, vandalism, not hearing when being spoken to, inappropriate laughing and joking, or an inability to move or speak. Compassionate and firm direction is critical to contain and guide the intense emotionalism of these young people in your school.

The time for restructuring the emotional equilibrium follows the initial shock and the ensuing fight-or-flight response and should focus on the children finding new meaning in life during the aftermath of tragedy. In devising a plan, attention must be given to the intensity of this need for meaning, especially for those students in their adolescent years. On-going counseling and ready identification of teenagers struggling with this issue must be provided.

SHORT-TERM EFFECTS OF CRISIS

Physical Response:

1. Frozen in place: shock, disorientation, numbness
2. Fight-or-Flight response: adrenalin pumps, heart races, hyper-ventilation occurs
3. Exhaustion: when fight or flight can no longer be prolonged

Coinciding Emotional Response:

1. Shock: disbelief, denial
2. Cataclysm of emotions: anger/rage, fear/terror, grief/sorrow, confusion/self-doubt
3. Reconstruction of emotional equilibrium

LONG-TERM EFFECTS OF CRISIS

In most crises only a few children are affected over a long term. (It is seldom that a crisis will be so traumatic and affect so many that a widespread reaction occurs). For those who are seriously affected, arrangements must be made to provide follow-up support. For many, however, the "long term" effects discussed here only last for a few days or weeks.

Crisis Causes Loss

People live their lives based on certain assumptions which provide the foundation to help them make sense of the world and life events. When a tragedy strikes, these assumptions are shattered. It is the loss of these assumptions that makes restructuring necessary. The losses are:

- Loss of a sense of control over one's life
- Loss of trust in God and adults
- Loss of the sense of fairness
- Loss of a sense of well-being and invulnerability
- Loss of a sense of security
- Personal losses of people or property

The long-term effects are similar to the pattern of the individual's short-term reaction, only milder. For instance, if a child's major initial reaction is one of running away and physically removing himself from the scene of the incident, his long-term reaction will consist of various forms of running away: giggling when emotions are discussed, distracting himself in continuous activity and changing the conversation when the subject of the incident arises. It takes time and direction for teenagers to restore their assumptions and rebuild their foundations and it takes time for young children to trust and feel secure again.

Crisis Involving Violence

If the tragedy involved violence, the child may relive it in recurrent dreams which could lead to a fear of sleeping. As the restructuring continues, however, the dreams normally provide a rescuer. Flashbacks, which are frequently associated with a sense of guilt, may also occur. They are the reliving of an event in a waking state as if it were happening in the present. Children will also relive the event in repetitive play using themes relating to the trauma. All of these reactions are crucial to the restructuring of assumptions and the child should understand that these are normal. The child should also be encouraged to discuss them.

Observing Crisis Anniversaries

In your crisis planning, be attuned to the importance of anniversaries commemmorating the people killed in a tragic accident. If a crisis involving a senior occurs during the year, the student body and the parents will want to acknowledge the deceased at graduation. This will satisfy their need to find meaning in the student's life, and bring closure to the tragedy.

If the deceased student was a member of a team, any awards the team goes on to win must also involve a commemoration of that student's life. These affairs and anniversaries will trigger a reaction in the students and staff that should be discussed.

Loss of Academic Ability

During the aftermath of a crisis situation, the academic capability of the students most directly involved will be adversely affected. There will be a loss of recently acquired skills. No new lessons should be introduced to the students for three to five days unless absolutely necessary. If new material must be delivered, allow the students extra time to absorb it. A diminished interest in schoolwork is quite natural. When a student is trying to decipher what life means and why death occurs, factoring algebra becomes secondary.

After the initial distress of a traumatic event, a numbness sets in, providing a cushion to any further emotional impact on the psyche. Feelings are tuned out and confusion reigns. Long-range planning is impossible. There is a sense of a foreshortened future. The student cannot imagine life a year from now. This distraction phase is only temporary and an accurate sense of time and the ability to set goals will return.

Trauma is often accompanied by regression. Expect the students to act less mature than usual. Irritability and outbursts of anger will occur frequently and children will be easily provoked into fighting. Ironically, relationships will suffer because of this irritability at a time when support is needed most.

Recovery from these long-term effects is influenced by the ability to understand, in retrospect, what has happened. Once the storm is successfully weathered, the child will have built a repertoire for coping beyond his years. The legacy of crisis can be a richer, more productive life with a deepened sense of meaning.

BEHAVIOR TO EXPECT OF STUDENTS AND FACULTY

Immediate:

- Flight
- Avoidance by creating distractions
- Giggling
- Immobilization

Long-Term:

- Similar but milder reaction to trigger event
- Grief due to losses
- Flashbacks (often associated with guilt)
- Recurrent dreams and fear of sleeping
- Repetitive play with themes of trauma
- Avoidance of reminders
- Amnesia
- Loss of recently acquired skills
- Diminished interest
- Numbed feelings
- Sense of foreshortened future
- Outbursts of anger
- Concentration impairment
- Hyperventilation
- Reactions at time of anniversary of event

UNDERSTANDING GRIEF

Often the students who exhibit the most behavioral and emotional problems and who have a difficult time adjusting academically and socially are the children who have suffered a serious loss in their personal lives. For four years, counselors in the 143 schools in Duval County, Florida documented the problems they were addressing in counseling. It was found that 65% of the children they were seeing had already experienced a major loss in their lives. Seeing these troubled children individually and in groups provides the support they need to cope with such devastating losses. Counselors already have many of the skills necessary to work with these children and, since most schoolwide tragedies involve death or major loss, these individual counseling experiences will prepare the counselor with skills and confidence.

Five Stages of the Grief Reaction

It is important to understand the emotional reactions of the normal grief cycle and that conceptualizing grief in stages is convenient for teaching purposes. In real life, however, every person grieves somewhat differently and there is seldom any clear-cut order or pattern. One child might move quickly from one emotion to another while a second child might exhibit only one intense emotion over a long period of time. Both reactions are normal. With this in mind, the five generally recognized stages in a grief reaction are: *denial, fear, anger, depression,* and *reorganization.* Because each stage is usually accompanied by identifiable behaviors, specific activities appropriate to each behavior are included at the end of Part III

The Denial Stage

The denial experienced after a significant loss is the psyche's natural protection at work, preventing too much emotional impact from occurring all at once. The person, intellectually aware that a death has occurred, *feels* that the deceased will be back. Many people experience seeing a stranger on the street who, for a brief moment, they mistakenly identify as the deceased. They may act as if the person will return. Parents often leave a bedroom of a deceased son or daughter exactly as it was when the child died. They will not empty the room or change it until they have the courage to admit the child will not return.

Making Deals

People make bargains with God. A child may say in prayer, "If I get all A's on my report card, will you bring Daddy back?" Hoping to gain back a lost love, a child will struggle for a few months to do everything he feels is expected of him and becomes a "model" child. Adults are amazed at how well he seems to be handling the tragedy. This effort is not sustained, however, and the child soon realizes the bargain is one-sided. The grieving period then begins and is usually accompanied by inconsistent behavior.

This period of denial normally lasts a few weeks to several months before the child begins to grieve. If a child expresses a belief in the loved one's return, do not refute it. You will be closing the door to further communication. It is best to identify the emotion felt. You may say, "You really miss your dad now," or "You must really be wishing he'd return." Eventually the child's own conversation and your understanding and acceptance will assist him through the grief.

Immediately following a death or a serious incident, the child may not wish to talk about it. Accept this refusal but remind the child that when the time comes, you will be there to listen. If the child is doing well academically and socially, there is no need to intervene, even if the denial period lasts for a long time.

Fantasy Beliefs

The story of Jane is somewhat typical of long-term denial. Jane was a junior in high school when her mother died of cancer. Although she helped to care for her mother prior to the death, Jane exhibited no emotional reaction even at the time of death. She continued to lead an active social life, dating, performing well academically, and remaining involved in school activities. During this time, however, unknown to anyone else, she firmly believed her mother was in Europe shopping for her. After she graduated from high school, Jane remained on a stable course until age twenty. She then began grieving for her mother and sought counseling. It was at this time that Jane realized how determined she had been to be "normal," seeking to live her teenage years with a mother like everyone else.

When to Intervene

Jane had functioned well and no intervention was necessary even though her denial lasted a long time. If, however, during the denial stage, a child begins to show erratic behavior, hostility, depression, or a marked drop in grades, it would be time to intervene.

Intervention should include activity that has some continuity. One approach is to work with the child on a scrapbook containing photographs or magazine clippings reminiscent of the deceased. The pictures provide a symbolic way to retain the closeness so badly missed and they help to replace the emptiness. This activity also gives the child an avenue to express some of the emotions felt because of this loss. More importantly, the child slowly begins to see the difference between what is now and what was then. This stage of resolution can also be achieved with artwork, having the child draw pictures comparing the "used to be's" and the "nows."

Using Commemoratives to Remember

When a loved one dies, a bewildering emptiness is often experienced by the survivor. An intimacy has been wrenched away generating feelings of loss and confusion. Helping the child find a commemorative of the deceased loved one can often help to fill the void, especially if it can be carried. When six-year-old Cindy's grandmother died, Cindy lost a friend. Because Cindy's parents both worked, her grandmother had been the one who helped get Cindy and her brother off to school everyday. After the death, Cindy began to carry a washcloth to school and hold onto it throughout the day. At first it was overlooked but after a few days the teacher became concerned and questioned Cindy about it. Cindy told her that the last thing her grandmother did to her before school each day was wash her face with a washcloth. Cindy was not ready to let go of her grandmother and this was her way of remaining close. This was accepted by the teacher and after a few months Cindy seldom brought the washcloth to school. No issue was ever made of this and Cindy gradually accepted life without her grandmother.

Solace in Dreams

Dreams can often speak to an individual when consciousness will not. The grieving process is often filled with dreams of the deceased person. Having a student keep track of these dreams pictorially or through a dream diary will help the child feel the presence of the relationship and slowly acknowledge the absence of the person.

The Fear Stage

A serious tragedy, such as the death of a parent, instills a far more intense fear in children than does a minor loss as when a pet dies. A crisis involving violence will also provoke fear. When the parent of a student dies, it may be necessary to address the classmates as well as the child involved since the others may have fears that their own parents may die. With most children, reassurance through discussion can usually alleviate this problem.

Fear for the Surviving Parent

For the child whose parent has died, the feeling frequently occurs that something tragic may also happen to the other parent. The child tends to hide his/her own grief in an effort to protect that remaining parent on whom there is such dependency. It is not unusual for a child, particularly a young child, to develop what looks like a school phobia. Refusing to attend school, making excuses to stay home, and missing the school bus are all active efforts to remain close to the parent for just a few more moments. This is not a school phobia developing. It is a fear that the remaining parent will not be there when the child returns home from school. Usually a child returns to school the day after the funeral. If there is a particular reluctance to leave home, allowing a child to remain home for a few more days my prevent such a reac-

PRAYER OF THE FROG

Dear God,
Why am I so small?
Why am I so green?
During the day will I live?
During the night will I die?
It was day but now it's night,
And, God, thanks for not letting me get stepped on.
But how long will I live during the day or the night?
 (I hope long). Amen.

This poem was written as a class assignment by a third-grader whose father had recently died and who had observed a frog trapped between the panes of a sliding glass door. The fear this child experienced can be seen in his sensitivity to the frog's plight.

tion. During this time, the out-of-state relatives will leave and neighbors will no longer bring food for dinner. Life will return to a degree of normalcy. With a settled routine at home, the child can feel more secure about returning to school.

Coping with grief is like riding an emotional roller coaster; up and in control, then down and out of control. Some days a survivor feels competent. On other days, confusion, anger, and hopelessness may take over. On those days that are difficult for the child, perhaps on the first day back to school, a telephone reassurance program can be established. If the child is inattentive in class or appears upset, encourage a call to the parent. The parent can give the child an upbeat message such as "We'll have pizza for dinner and watch TV together tonight. I'll see you in a little while." Comforted by the sureness in the parent's voice and the normal activity spoken about on the phone, the child will then return to class feeling much easier about being there.

Provide Assurance of Care

One of the most serious questions on a child's mind after the loss of a parent is, "If this parent also leaves or dies, who will take care of me?" After such an experience, children know the adults in their life are not in total control of all eventualities. Parents have a responsibility to ensure their children's survival and must make arrangements to assure this is done in the event of their death. They can let the child know of these arrangements in a reassuring way by saying, "More than likely, I'll be around to see my grandchildren, but just so you don't have to worry, this is who will take care of you if something should happen to me." Although the parent should remain responsive to follow-up questions, it is not necessary to dwell on the subject.

When a tragedy occurs involving an act of violence, such as a shooting in the school, the fear generated may be alleviated by focusing discussion on ways to protect oneself and each other. Calling in experts such as Officer Friendly to give safety instructions will have an additional impact.

Develop the "Rescue" Outcome

Many children will experience nightmares after violence. Discussion of these nightmares helps. Telling stories of good overcoming evil restores the child's faith in his world. In one case, after a shooting of a teacher in an elementary school, the pictures drawn by the students involved "rescuers." They actually changed the outcome, providing an alternative they could more readily handle. This type of activity can be directed and children can be encouraged to create the ending they wished had happened.

A group of children aged seven to eleven were discussing the recent suicide of a ten-year-old neighbor; "If I were there, I would have . . ." Once into this subject, the children became more animated and one could see how they were beginning to restore their sense of control over their environment.

Intellectual Approach

Help older students use their intellects to challenge the irrational fears that frequently develop. Albert Ellis' A-B-C approach to rational thinking is a wonderful tool that teaches teenagers a system of coping with fears by providing their own internal reassurance that will serve them well for a lifetime. This strategy can be learned from Ellis's *A New Guide to Rational Thinking.*

The Anger Stage

When a tragedy occurs, anger is the dominant emotion you will encounter with the students. There are times when the tragedy provides a target for the anger as in the case of a child struck by a drunken driver. While it is easy to believe the anger is justifiably and rightfully directed at the target, the source of the anger is deeper and the anger would be there even if there were no direct target. The students will search for someone or something to blame and thereby justify their angry attacks.

Anger is one of the normal emotions of grief any survivor feels. For young people, especially teenagers, it is the sudden shattering of the assumptions they live by that lies at the root of their anger. This must first be accepted and validated. They must know that they are normal, that the anger is justified, and that it will dissipate over time if given an avenue of expression.

Directing Anger Into Constructive Activities

As a counselor, most of the work you will be doing with the students is helping to direct this anger into constructive activities. The students should be taught that while they may not be able to control their feelings of anger which are often irrational, what they do with their anger, how they channel it, is THEIR responsibility. When students learn to direct their anger into a productive activity, they will use this new coping skill throughout their lives because this event and the activities following it will never be forgotten.

Physical and Creative Activities

How do you decide which activities will work? First, determine the particular character of the student. Students who are very physical, get restless easily, and move fast everywhere they go will handle anger more naturally in an aggressive manner. For them, physical release is best. Have them run around the school yard, compete with others, arm wrestle, swim laps in the pool, pound a punching bag, or dance. Students who are more sedentary or creative can finger paint, knead clay for pottery, hammer, build something, write letters, keep a journal or compose a poem. An oral release works well for the child whose usual method of dealing with anger is to yell or become sarcastic. Give this child an opportunity to talk a lot, sing aloud with gusto, speak into a tape recorder, or scream when he is alone.

One ten-year-old, who lost his sister in an accident, became verbally abusive to his teacher, classmates, and his parent. To help him, we gave him a tape recorder and challenged him to create the "grossest" stories he could. He was able to express his anger through detailed accounts of what different characters he created did to each other. Within a week he exhibited decidedly fewer aggressive verbal attacks. Once an appropriate outlet was provided and he was reminded to use this outlet to ventilate, he discontinued the verbal abuse of other people.

Group Discussions

Use group discussions to urge students to share their methods of dealing with anger and the consequences of those ways. Encourage them to explore creative and productive new ways to release anger. The group can focus on one common group activity or experiment with different ways of individually handling anger. If the group opts for individual activities, follow up, using peer group appraisal and approval to reinforce the new behaviors.

The Depression Stage

Perhaps the longest stage a survivor must endure is depression which in young people is exhibited by either of two types of behavior. In the first type, most often associated with depression, the person cries frequently, is lethargic, withdraws from activities and lacks initiative. The second type of behavior, caused by but not generally associated with depression, is often misinterpreted. It is the "running away" or avoidance behavior seen in the student who cannot be serious, who becomes a "party person" and who may distract himself through substance abuse and promiscuity. Such activities are an attempt to avoid facing depressed and empty feelings.

Depression as a Healthy Response

Depression following death serves a purpose. It is the psyche's way of protecting itself from too much emotional impact. Tragedy occurring in the life of a young person devastates any ability to cope with the changes incurred, let alone any emotional energy needed to progress. A student will not try out for the track team because the psyche cannot afford any possible emotional rejection. Depression is an insulation from risk-taking by allowing only certain things to be of great importance in life. This is helpful because it gives time to heal and rest.

Depression as a Problem

Depression develops into a problem if the person becomes self-deprecating in reaction to this current subdued level of functioning. Feelings of inadequacy may set in. It is easy for the depressed person to lose perspective and feel the depression will last forever. A sense of self-worth can diminish tremendously at this time. Frequent reminders must be given that all things change and that the melancholia will also change.

The counselor should also help the student to find and build the strength he used in the past. Remind him that strength is still with him even though he may not at present believe it. Work with the student to discover if anger has been adequately expressed. Oftentimes depression is anger turned inward and it becomes a way of punishing oneself for real or imagined deeds. Help the depressed student to continue functioning, but do not expect the same normal achievement level. Most importantly, arrange for the student to help someone else. This will prevent self-pity and bolster self-esteem.

A depressed person is generally avoided by other people. When depression occurs in a child, that child will receive less recognition and nurturing than is needed. This is truly sad because praise and nurturing are essential for recovery from depression. Giving praise and nurture is not an easy task, however, since a depressed person does little for which to be commended. Barely perceptible positive behavior must be noticed and acknowledged.

When people feel a sense of tragedy and become speechless, it is because words are truly inadequate to the experience. Many times in the depths of depression, the most comforting thing a person can experience is a hug or a pat on the back. This is especially true for a depressed child. Touch communicates nurture to a child in a way no words ever could. It assures the child that someone does care, that there is some strength and stability in a world that seems shattered, and it provides the hope of an understanding person to talk to later when it's time to talk about it.

The Reorganization Stage

With the passage of time, emotional healing and equilibrium normally return and the mourning ends. Some people, however, fear that if they cease mourning, they will no longer remember the person. They have already realized that dreams of the deceased occur less frequently and they find it difficult to remember exactly what the deceased looked like—the image of his or her face is no longer clear.

Before these people can once again organize their lives, they need permission to cease mourning, permission to continue living. If the person is unable to do this, the permission must come from another trusted person. Within the school, that trusted person is oftentimes a school counselor or favored teacher.

A Ritual to End Mourning

The funeral gives closure to the life of the deceased, but there is no ritual in our society to give closure to the period of mourning. To integrate effectively the experience of the mourning period and resume life with meaning and joy, a ritual of farewell or goodbye is necessary. The ritual must be personal and decided by the individual. It may be as small as a conversation of goodbye with the deceased or as involved as building a memorial to the loved one. Here again, the task of helping the child discover a ritual falls naturally on the counselor.

The Relationship Continues

Besides finding a satisfying ritual, the grieving child needs to be reassured that giving up the mourning does not mean giving up the relationship. Whether present or not, a child's father will always be that child's father. This child can retain the continuity of the relationship by selecting a quality

A NEW FRAME OF THOUGHT

I see a dark, dank scum around the windows
A broken down roof and tattered walls.
I place my hand gently
  on an old, frail mirror
And small, dainty pieces begin to fall
  onto a shambled, wooden floor.
They land with off-key harmony
  into a cloud of hazy dust.
A broken-down rocking horse,
   alone in the corner,
    just left in the attic to rust.
I close my eyes
No draft I feel.
This giant scrapbook of memories
  is stuffy, and preserved
Smelling of antique, sawdust air
  with other scents sitting to be stirred.

It's time, I say to you now,
For the windows to be opened up wide.
My head must be cleared.
I've now no feelings to hide.
There's a cool, calm breeze in my attic
And my rocking horse starts to sing.
I gently place my hand on a delicate mirror
No glass broken, everything
  shimmering,
   shimmering,
    shimmering.

This poem was written by Amy Mayer, age 16, depicting her recovery from her parents' divorce and a move to another state. Used with permission.

or skill most admired in the deceased and incorporating it into his/her own life. The example of a fourteen-year-old teenager comes to mind. After the death of his grandfather, whom he loved dearly, the young man was reminded by his counselor of the grandfather's patience while teaching the proper use of tools in the workshop. The young man chose to learn patience in an effort to incorporate and retain a vital part of the relationship he experienced with his grandfather.

STAGES OF GRIEF

Denial/Shock

- Feeling of numbness
- Belief or feeling that deceased will return
- Insomnia/sleeplessness
- Loss of appetite (people literally forget to eat)
- Inconsistent behavior
- Bargaining with God
- Persistent dreams or nightmares
- Inability to concentrate
- Preoccupation without being able to identify with what
- Confusion

Fear

- Nightmares
- Sleeplessness
- Easily startled
- Anxiety and restlessness
- Verbal expressions of false bravado
- Phobias

Anger

- Irritability
- Provocative in fights
- Sarcastic remarks
- Anti-social behavior
- Vandalism
- Refusal to comply with rules

Guilt

- Often masked by anger
- Self-destructive behavior

- Apologetic attitude
- Acting out in response to praise or compliments

Depression

two patterns observed especially in young people.

Typical Depression

- Lethargy
- Decreased attention span
- Frequent crying
- Unkempt appearance
- Disintereset in activities
- Suicidal thoughts
- Withdrawal from friends
- Overeating or loss of appetite
- Self-deprecation
- Oversleeping or inability to sleep

Masking Depression

- Substance abuse
- Consistent restlessness
- Consistent inappropriate joking
- Involvement in high-risk behaviors
- Gains reputation of "party person"
- Sexual promiscuity
- Adoption of an "I don't care" attitude

Reorganization

- Dreams of deceased become infrequent
- Joy and laughter return
- Planning for future begins
- Reinvestment in activities once dropped or forgotten

GRIEF COUNSELING

After walking the path of a child's grief, sharing this final stage is one of the most rewarding times a counselor will experience. After the ritual of good-bye, the child resumes a healthy emotional life and once again becomes invested in activities and other people around him. Timing for the ritual closure is important, however, and cannot be rushed. If an extremely close relationship existed between the individuals, it may take two or more years before the final goodbye can occur.

Validation and Coping Skills

Grief counseling differs from other counseling in that much of it is not goal-oriented. There is seldom confrontation. Listening and validating the experience is the major part of your work with a grieving child. Helping the child select and use effective coping skills to handle the intense emotions is a vital part of the counseling and should be addressed directly. A statement such as "Okay, you're angry and that's natural. Let's find ways that you can release that anger and not get into trouble" validates the emotion, offers assistance in handling this anger, and places the responsibility of the behavior on the child. Although grief counseling is a lengthy process, it does not have to be time-consuming. For a few weeks initially, a child may need frequent attention but usually only for brief periods of time. Ten minutes at the moment of distress is worth hours of counseling after the fact. As time goes on this child may need counseling only occasionally although counseling could easily continue for a full school year.

When a tragedy occurs within the school community, it is imperative that the emotional needs of the students, faculty, and other staff are tended to before the academic schedule resumes. The Guidance Department must be prepared with a program to handle the situation and the program should receive the full support of the administration. The emotional stages—denial, fear, anger, depression—experienced by the individuals affected by the tragedy are necessary in helping the psyche to adjust, heal, and reorganize itself.

POST TRAUMATIC STRESS DISORDER

It is a rare person who lives a life free of unexpected loss. If the loss results from an abrupt accident or violent action, the aftershock can last for years. In appearance and action, the individual experiencing this aftershock may seem to have an almost robot-like demeanor, lacking the vitality and spirit indicative of a healthy human being. The smile given is with the mouth only and the body performs functions routinely without a hint of zest or exuberance. Participation in positive, healthy activities is exceptional whereas unhealthy, negative behavior is more common. A withdrawal to the self occurs and can be accomplished by drinking or indulgence in other drugs. A Post Traumatic Stress Disorder (PTSD) is in process.

The perception of violence is that it occurs relatively infrequently in society and only occasionally at school. Statistics are scarce but evidence of increasing violence is demonstrated in today's headlines and newscasts.

Violence or its threat can result in serious emotional reactions that, if left unresolved, can lead to Post Traumatic Stress Disorder. If 25 percent of adults who suffer a traumatic or violent loss go through PTSD, one can imagine how high that statistic must be for children, although there is no evidence through research to substantiate any figure.

Post Traumatic Stress Disorder is a common human problem that has received public attention only recently in the aftermath of the Vietnam war. It is a normal response to an abnormal event, but it can be devastatingly disruptive for years. In many cases, however, it can be prevented.

Recognizing the Symptoms

It is important to recognize the symptoms, understand why they occur and be aware of some steps you can take to prevent PTSD in the aftermath of a crisis. As educators and guidance counselors, you are not in the position to attempt to cure, although you need to know when to refer a student for professional help. Prevention is always best, however, and you are in an excellent position to take the proper action.

Certain incidents more readily precipitate PTSD. They are:

- The death of or serious harm to a close friend
- The suicide of a friend
- The inability to help in a situation when no one else is present to do so
- Hostage situations
- Witnessing violence
- Particularly gruesome events
- The panic and hysteria following a tragedy
- Heavy media attention

If students in your school have faced these events on any one particular day, begin a defusing before they leave school that very day. Basically, this process involves the ventilating of thoughts and emotions after a crisis. Then

SYMPTOMS OF POST TRAUMATIC STRESS DISORDER

- Recurrent and intrusive recollections of the event
- Nightmares
- Numbing of emotions
- Marked disinterest in activities
- Feelings of detachment
- Hypervigilant or avoidace-behavior
- Decline in cognitive performance
- Startled reactions
- Overwhelming and persistent guilt
- Attacks of shallow breathlessness, heart palpitations, sweating, shaking

Symptoms Specific to Children

- Distortion of time concerning the incident
- Distortion of the sequence of events
- Retrospective identification of supposed premonitions
- Reenactments of traumatic events (usually not conscious)
- Repetitive play involving traumatic themes
- Pessimistic expectations of the future and lifespan
- Marked and enduring personality changes
- Greater memory of the event than adults
- Fantasizing changes to "undo" the event

debrief those same students several days later, continuing weekly until the students have had the chance to integrate the experience into their lives and restructure their beliefs about the world. This usually takes about three months. This timely attention will go a long way toward the prevention of PTSD. The specific procedure for defusing and debriefing is covered at the end of this chapter under PREVENTING POST TRAUMATIC STRESS DISORDER. Reactions to trauma-inducing incidents occur in three phases:

The Impact Phase

The Impact phase occurs immediately following an event and can last minutes or days. During this phase, the person is either functioning mechanically (on "automatic") or is so stunned he cannot act at all. Denial of the effects is common, especially among men and boys with a macho attitude. The intensity of the effects is increased when the media is involved because of their focus on the distress of the individuals rather than the event. When attorneys and police are involved, anxiety is heightened even further.

The Recoil Phase

The Recoil phase can last a few days to several weeks. There is a great need to retell the story during this time. People will also become overreactive, particularly to any reminders of the event, such as a loud noise after a shooting, or a heavy rain following a devastating hurricane. The emotional reactions begin during this phase and angry outbursts, bouts of uncontrollable crying, and panic attacks can occur.

Onset of Post Traumatic Stress Disorder

The actual onset of the PTSD phase begins weeks or even months after the event has occurred. People will feel a great sense of grief not only for whatever losses may have been sustained but also for the collapse of their assumptions and beliefs about the world. Survivor guilt is usually present, especially when a person benefits from the disaster.

For example, in one school, a young man accidentally shot his girlfriend. He had not been particularly popular prior to the event and in an effort to console him, his classmates reached out to him. Several girls, caught in the web of excitement, were attracted to him and made their feelings obvious. His popularity had suddenly increased and he felt excrutiatingly guilty realizing he had benefited from the "killing" of his friend.

In cases involving victimization, there is usually an acute sense of helplessness that must be overcome. The necessary restoration of self-confidence is actually achieved through one of the most troublesome symptoms, the intrusive thoughts. Replaying the incident over and over is the mind's attempt to make senes of what happened and thereby gain a sense of mastery over the event. Phobias and anxiety, sometimes directly related to the experience but more often a free-floating generalized uneasiness, persist because a basic trust in the world has been shattered.

A person suffering from PTSD will usually undergo severe interruptions in relationships. This is because the integration of a traumatic experience is internal and intense and not easily shared with someone who was not there. The emotional backlash resulting from this destruction of trust and values is frequently vented on the closest friends and family.

Shattered Assumptions

Victimization or watching someone being victimized shatters the assumptions with which we all build our lives. The destruction of these assumptions provides fertile ground for PTSD; there are several which we need to consider more closely.

The Assumption of Invulnerability

Although news of shootings, accidents, and disasters are presented to us with every newscast, we live under the assumption that these calamities will not strike us. This sense of invulnerability provides a natural protection from stress and anxiety. However, when an incident occurs that shatters this assumption, we must change our beliefs to include the facts that 1) it can happen to me, and 2) the world is not as safe as I thought it was.

Preoccupation with the fear that anything can happen reflects the victim's new and intense feeling of vulnerability. The self-concept changes to accept and perpetuate the role of the victim. The perception of the world as a benign place changes because the victim has experienced a malevolent world. Those who have felt the most invulnerable before an event occurs have the most difficult time adjusting, because the event shatters truisms that have never been questioned. It is no wonder that teenagers are so vulnerable to psychological disruption after a traumatic event.

Assumption that the World is Meaningful

Meaning in the world centers on the belief that there is a natural order, a way of things are "supposed" to happen, and that this natural order is understandable. A crisis involving victimization destroys the "order" of things and does not make sense. When victimization occurs, people must reconstruct the order and find purpose in the event. After experiencing a tragedy, people will often dedicate themselves to fight any wrongdoing in their effort to make the world "right" again. Mothers against Drunk Drivers (MADD) and Students Against Drunk Drivers (SADD) are perfect examples.

One young paramedic readily remembers the day she chose her career. She was sixteen and riding on the highway with her grandfather. They were the first to arrive at an accident in which a baby had been thrown from a car and the parents and two other children were still trapped inside. The grandfather picked up the baby and gave it to the young girl while he tried to free the others. The girl did not know what to do with the baby. Other motorists stopped and offered no assistance. This sixteen-year-old girl watched the baby die in her arms that day and swore that she would never let that happen again.

She decided then to become a paramedic so that next time she would know what to do.

This young girl restored her teenage idealism with the promise, "I will never let this happen again." She also restored her sense of meaning by believing that learning how to help save lives gave some purpose to the death of the baby in her arms. She answered the important question, "Why did this happen to me?"

Assumptions of Self-Image

People who believe that they operate in a relatively safe world formulate an image of themselves and others as benevolent. When this image is violated, victims need to feel less vulnerable and will seek to make sense of what happened by assigning accountability and determining who is responsible for the event. It is ironic but true that victims who decide they did something which allowed the incident to happen are actually restoring a personal sense of control. For instance, when a violent attack occurs and victims see themselves as merely passive recipients of the act, they must live with the thought that it can happen again. However, if victims assign themselves some responsibility by believing, for instance, "I shouldn't have walked in that neighborhood at night," they can identify a behavior to change, thus restoring a sense of control and reducing anxiety.

In this manner, victims can still see themselves in a favorable way by affirming, "I am a decent person. . . there are some bad people in the world. . . I know what to do to stay away from those people." The victims thereby maintain a sense of control.

Coping Strategies

After a tragic occurrence, there are coping strategies that help restore faith and trust in oneself, other people and the world.

Redefining the Event

Nowhere is the redefining of an event more obvious than in young children. They will unabashedly change their story as time goes on. A group of children, aged six to eleven, had witnessed the aborted attempt at resuscitating a ten-year-old who had hanged himself. To them the issue of assigning responsibility was paramount. The discussion shifted from who was to blame, to why did he do it, to the feelings of anger and sadness over the death. The children finally decided it was really an accident, that the victim didn't know what could happen and that he only wanted to scare his mother. They then began to talk about what they would have done to save him if they had been allowed. In so doing they redefined the event, assigned causality that could have been avoided, and restored their own sense of control after experiencing the helplessness of watching heroic but unsuccessful efforts.

Finding Meaning

After a traumatic event, people frequently are preoccupied for months or even years asking the question, "Why?" Although there really isn't an answer to this question, the process of the search for an answer is vital to restoring the meaning. Eventually some people will find themselves sensitive to a particular issue and will start to devote a great deal of energy to it. Later they will assign meaning to the tragedy by aligning it with the endeavor they chose. Other persons may search for a cause to champion and consciously assign meaning to the tragedy through the good they bring to the world. This reestablishes a person's belief in the order of the universe.

Changing Behaviors

Another method of recovery is to identify those behaviors that originally led to a crisis and change them. These direct actions provide the victims with a sense of control over their environment and decrease their feelings of vulnerability. These changes in behavior also increase self-esteem because the victims see themselves no longer allowing any victimization. The actions taken involve practical preventive steps to decrease the likelihood of the event reoccurring. After a mugging, they may decide to take alternate routes and learn self-defense; after an accident while drinking, to never drink and drive again.

Seeking Social Support

Although turning to others is a natural reaction, many people find the world less than supportive in the aftermath of a crisis. Sometimes the event is so traumatic that non-involved people do not want to feel that they themselves might be that vulnerable and so they withhold the support they would like to extend. Then the best support will come from peers who have experienced the same or a similar event. This is why it is so essential that defusing takes place at school, if at all possible, before releasing the children.

The peer support groups help to normalize a reaction which, through its intensity, appears "crazy." People are so unprepared for the normal reactions to these abnormal situations that their own reactions are as frightening to them as is the situation they have just experienced. Social support must be "unconditionally available" if it is to restore a benevolent view of life. This is vital since any negative tone or unavailability of support confirms the victims' questioning of their own self-worth and spawns a victim mentality.

TRAUMA IN CHILDHOOD DEVELOPMENTAL DIFFERENCES

Preschool and Kindergarten

- Extremely sensitive to trauma
- Play a passive role in the face of trauma
  —cannot imagine what to do
  —flee, look away, or observe detached
- Imagine superheroes protecting them
- Often mute about the event
- Reenact trauma in play
- Excessive clinging behavior and separation anxiety
- Toileting accidents
- Autoerotic activity
- Sleep disturbances
- Increased aggressive conduct

Elementary School Age

- Dullness
- Decreased intellectual functioning
- Decline in school performance
- Decreased ability to focus and concentrate
- Decreased spontaneous thought in an effort to decrease intrusive thoughts of traumatic event
- Focus on imagined actions they wished they had taken
- Play-acting the role of hero
- Fantasizing revenge
- Persistent focus on details of the trauma
- Trouble with peer relationships
- Change in personality
  —exuberant child becomes withdrawn, unspontaneous
  —quiet child becomes rude, irritable, aggressive
- Decreased trust in adults' ability to protect
- Psychosomatic complaints

Adolescents

- Premature entry into adulthood
- Premature closing of identity formation
- Sensitive to feelings of shame and being stigmatized
- Acting out behavior very common
  —truancy
  —precocious sexual activity
  —substance abuse
  —delinquency
- Occasional reenactment behavior which is life-threatening due to
  —accessibility of cars and weapons
  —poor impulse control
- Self-destructive behavior
- Suspicious and guarded demeanor with everyone
- Judgmental and unforgiving of their own behavior and that of others
- Guilt-ridden due to disappointment in their own behavior during the crisis
- Ability to anticipate the effects of the trauma on their lives

PREVENTING POST TRAUMATIC STRESS DISORDER

The following set of procedures should be offered to both staff and students. It consists of two parts:

1. Defusing—the ventilation of thoughts and emotions immediately following a tragic event. The students/staff exposed to the incident must talk with each other prior to leaving that day.
2. Debriefing—begins the process of putting the incident and the individuals' reactions in perspective. This can be done in three days to two weeks after the event.

The staff can be involved in the defusing/debriefing process for student but students should not be included in the staff defusing/debriefing.

Defusing

These are the steps to be taken in the defusing:

- Provide information and include parents if they come to school
- Keep everyone together for sometime (groups of 15–20)
- Promote ventilation:
  Ask: What was the worst part for you?
      Where were you when it happened?
      (Listen! Listen! Listen!)
- Prepare students and parents for reactions of:
  —sleeplessness　　　　　　—fear and anxiety
  —lack of concentration　　—nightmares
  —nausea　　　　　　　　—sweating
  —crying　　　　　　　　—numbness
  —irritability　　　　　　—withdrawing
  —demanding　　　　　　—clinging
- Let them know that they are normal
- Give them suggestions for coping
- Let them know when follow-up will be provided

Debriefing

There are the steps to be taken in the debriefing:

- Limit group to no more than 15–20.
- No family members are present
- Stress confidentiality
- Advise everyone to be themselves: to talk if they want, to not talk if they prefer to be silent
- Remind them that what they have to say may help someone else.

There will be a flow in the debriefing which will allow participants to begin to get involved emotionally at their own pace. The debriefing includes several phases which, once started, cannot be interrupted, even if it must go beyond class time.

Phase I—Information phase

- What happened?
- Where were you?
- What role did you play?

Phase II—Idea phase

- What thoughts have you had?
- What ideas did you think of?

Phase III—Emotional phase

- How did you react at first?
- How are you reacting now?
- What impact has this had on you? (Allow and encourage emotional expression: crying, anger, fear, etc.)

Phase IV—Meaning phase

- What repercussions has this had on your life?
- What symptoms are you experiencing?
- How has this affected your family? school? health? friends?

Phase V—Educational phase

- How have you coped with difficulties before?
- What are you doing to cope now?

Closure—

- Remind students of strengths
- Reassure them that it will take time to heal
- Reassure them that you will be there.

PART IV

ACTIVITIES FOR THE RESOLUTION OF TRAUMA AND GRIEF

Introduction

THIS SECTION PROVIDES thirty-two activities for students at different levels for use in individual, group and class settings. They were written to be easily accessed when you need them. Background information on crisis counseling and children's reactions to trauma and grief can be found in Part III.) If you have limited experience in leading groups, you may be especially interested in reading "You Can Do a Group," which appears at the beginning of the activities for groups and classrooms.

ACTIVITY 1. TO HELP A CHILD THROUGH DENIAL (ALL AGES)

If the student believes the deceased will return:

- do not refute
- identify with the feeling by saying, "You must really be missing _____ now." or "You must be feeling very lonely."

If a child doesn't want to talk:

- an occasional reminder that the door is open: "Remember, I'm still here if you want to talk."

When misbehavior erupts:

Suggest activities with continuity:

- scrapbook of photos

- magazine clippings reminding the child of the deceased
- artwork portraying "way it was and the way it is now." (Include many areas: home, school, family, holidays, dinner)

For bewildering emptiness:

- help the child choose a symbol to keep with him/her as a reminder of the deceased
- record dreams—pictorially or in a dream diary

ACTIVITY 2. TO HELP ALLEVIATE THE FEAR OF VIOLENCE (ALL AGES)

If an individual is involved, have a counselor or the principal speak with the child.

If a group is involved, have "experts" speak with the class on safety issues:

- avoiding unfamiliar people
- walking together
- use of designated "safe places"
- what the community is doing to keep children safe
- ways to avoid conflict

ACTIVITY 3. TO RESTORE A SENSE OF TRUST AND CONTROL AFTER VIOLENCE (ALL AGES)

- read and discuss stories of good overcoming evil
- draw pictures of what happened and how the students wished it had ended
- hold a discussion or draw pictures of what the students would like to have done.

ACTIVITY 4. TO RELEASE ANGER IN CONSTRUCTIVE WAYS (ALL AGES)

Physical Student

- run around the classroom, the gymnasium, or the building during P.E.
- swim laps
- arm wrestle or compete with others in acceptable ways
- pound a punching bag or pillow
- dance
- hit a baseball/tennis ball, fantasizing a face on the ball

Sedentary or Creative Student

- finger paint
- knead clay for pottery
- hammer
- build something
- write letters that will never be sent
- compose songs
- write poetry

Verbal Student

- talk to someone
- create stories on tape recorder
- scream in a good place (alone, on the playground, in a closet, driving alone, in the shower, etc.)
- talk out loud as if the person were there
- write letters that are never sent and reread them
- sing with gusto

ACTIVITY 5. TO HELP A STUDENT WITH DEPRESSION (ALL AGES)

- structure the student's assignments
- structure the student's life (see activity 6)
- praise often, even seemingly insignificant positive behavior
- hug when no words come
- have the student help someone else
- remind the student of successes and strengths of the past
- help the student organize by writing lists
- give frequent reassurance of hope: "This too shall pass"
- reduce your expectations of the student
- ask about suicide ideation (older children and teenagers)

ACTIVITY 6.
STRUCTURING ASSIGNMENTS AND LIFE
(UPPER ELEMENTARY AND SECONDARY)

THINGS I NEED TO DO:

Schoolwork: *Due by:*   *Steps to Take:*

_____

_____

_____

_____

Chores at Home: *Due by:*   *Steps to Take:*

_____

_____

_____

_____

For Others: *When:*   *Steps to Take:*

_____

_____

_____

_____

Things for Myself: *When:*   *Steps to Take:*

_____

_____

_____

_____

ACTIVITY 7. TO RE-ESTABLISH A SENSE OF CONTROL (PRIMARY GRADES)

Provide Toys

Make toys available to the children and encourage reenactment play with these toys. Dolls, puppets, boxes for buildings, cars, ambulances, and whatever other imaginative toys can duplicate the scene of the crisis. Encourage the children to find positive outcomes in their play. This will help them regain a sense of mastery over their lives.

ACTIVITY 8. TO HELP A CHILD DEAL WITH PAIN AND ANGER (ELEMENTARY)

Building Emotional Muscles

Have the child draw as large a picture of himself as he can and color the picture.

Discuss with the child:

- "Each time you feel hurt and let it out in a good way you build emotional muscles."
- "Each time you feel angry and let it out in a good way you build emotional muscles."
- "How can you let the hurt out in a good way? Do you talk to someone special? Do you draw pictures of the hurt? Do you ride your bicycle? (Explore until you and the child understand HIS/HER way of dealing with the pain in a productive fashion. If there is none, help select something that fits the child's situation.)
- "Everytime you use _____ to get out the pain, you color in more muscles on your body in your picture."

Repeat with the releasing of anger.

This exercise is more effective if continuity is established. If you do not have the time to spend in ongoing sessions with the child, ask about the muscles at every opportunity.

ACTIVITY 9. TO HELP A STUDENT DEAL WITH FEAR (UPPER ELEMENTARY AND JUNIOR HIGH)

Reassurance through discussion covering:

- what happens to the deceased
- how people survive a major loss
- reminders of the supportive people around
- reminders of strengths used in the past
- reading books together to promote discussion (see bibliography)

Telephone reassurance:

- have the child call a parent at home or work to reassure him/her that the parent is okay

Parent assistance:

- have a parent tell the child of arrangements for his/her care should the remaining parent not be available to care for the child

ACTIVITY 10. TO DETERMINE THE NUMBER AND SEVERITY OF CHANGES IN A STUDENT'S LIFE (UPPER ELEMENTARY AND SECONDARY)

Have the student begin to draw a straight line representing each year of his/her life.

For each time something good happened, have the student draw a mountain on the line and for each time something bad happened, have the student draw a valley on the line.

Example:

Determine the number of changes which have occurred in the student's life. Use this information to discuss how the student has coped with those past events and to determine if there are other areas of grief in his/her life besides the current traumatic event. The child must be validated for all these changes.

ACTIVITY 11. TO REPLACE A TRAUMATIC MEMORY WITH A POSITIVE ONE (SECONDARY)

This exercise is often used following the death of someone close to the student. Have the student relax and then follow with:

> Describe the image you see. [Have the student describe to you the traumatic image.] Now imagine that scene on a stage, and the curtain is closing on the scene. [Proceed slowly]
> Remember now a happy time with _____ . Describe in detail what you see. [Have the student describe to you the imagined scene and ask how warm or cool the environment is, how it feels, how it smells, and he/she feels.] Now keep this memory with you and everytime you want to bring it back as clear as it is right now, you can do that. Open your eyes when you are ready.

Instruct the student to replace the old image with the new happy image every time the traumatic image occurs. At first the student will have to struggle a little to keep the old image away but this can be accomplished by repeating the exercise. After a while it will be easier to replace and eventually the good image is the one that will be remembered.

ACTIVITY 12. TO HELP WITH LEAVING THE MOURNING PERIOD BEHIND (SECONDARY)

- Give the student permission to cease the mourning period
- Help the student choose a ritual of good-bye
- Remind the student that a relationship never ends
- Explore with the student what has been learned or can be learned from the life of the deceased
- Help the student plan how to make that memory a part of his/her own life
- Encourage a reinvestment in new or forgotten activities

ACTIVITY 13. TO EVALUATE SUICIDE SIGNS (UPPER ELEMENTARY AND SECONDARY)

Ask if the child thinks of suicide. If yes, find out how frequently:

- occasionally is normal
- every evening is serious

Ask if the child has decided how or when to commit suicide. If the child has an answer for this, get help immediately.

- The child who is upset, using drugs or alcohol, or under the influence should never be left alone.
- If the child knows someone who has committed suicide, the danger is increased.

ACTIVITY 14. TO INTERRUPT SUICIDAL THINKING (UPPER ELEMENTARY AND SECONDARY)

A suicide is not an impulsive act. A long time is needed to take action on suicidal thinking because the person is ambivalent about choosing life or death. It is important to emphasize life to the suicidal person and thus stop the ambivalence. To strengthen the choice for life, ask the student:

- "Tell me about the place in you that wants to live. How big is it? Is it bruised? Can it heal? Tell me more about the part of you that wants to live?"
- "What will happen if you die? To you? To others?" (Look for magical thinking here and challenge unrealistic ideas.)

Offer practical assistance to problem-solving:

- help the child to list his problems with you
- you write them down
- discuss and write down solutions to the problems (usually only two or three are unsolvable)
- if a call needs to be made you make the call
- if tutoring needs to be set up, you set it up (this is a time to unburden a student, not teach responsibility)

- when you reach the problems which cannot be solved (living in an alcoholic family, for example), explore coping skills and set up a program for the child to strengthen those skills.

When a suicide is imminent:

- do not leave the student alone
- get professional help
- tap into the desire to live (do not stop talking even if you repeat important messages—you do not want to give the message that you also ran out of things to do. Realize that a person on the brink of suicide hears only isolated words and phrases).
- challenge magical thinking
- give practical assistance

ACTIVITY: 15. TO HELP OVERCOME IRRATIONAL FEARS AND DEMANDS (SECONDARY LEVEL)

Albert Ellis's A-B-C Exercise

This exercise needs a brief explanation before implementation. It is adapted from Albert Ellis's Rational-Emotive Therapy in which *A* refers to an action or event that occurs; *B* is the belief or self-talk (all the things we say to ourselves in evaluating how and what we are doing) we have about the event; and *C* is the consequential reaction, both behavioral and emotional, we have as a result of this belief.

In other words, It is not the event itself that causes the reaction but what we say to ourselves about the event. For example, several students fail a test. One student reacts with devastation, another reacts by blaming the teacher and another reacts by studying harder for the next test. It is not the test that created these reactions, but rather what the students are saying to themselves.

The student who was devastated (*C*) says: "I'm always so stupid, I cannot learn." (*B*)

The student who blamed the teacher (*C*) says: "She doesn't like me, that's why she failed me." (*B*)

The student who decided to study more (*C*) says: "I guess I just didn't study enough; next time I will." (*B*)

This method especially applies to trauma reaction when a student is avoiding something as a result of the trauma, fears excessively that it may happen again or feels extreme guilt about some event.

HELP THE STUDENT by placing the event under *A*, then list under *C* the behavior and feelings generated in reaction to the event. Next have the student explore those things he/she is saying and internalizing and list under *B*.

To change the reaction, ask the student what reaction he/she would like to have and again list under *C*. Explore what he/she would have to say and internalize in order to have that reaction. Recommend that he/she practice saying those new things frequently.

A ACTION	B BELIEF	C CONSEQUENCE

Irrational Belief Systems

(Adapted from Albert Ellis's Rational-Emotive Therapy)

The following are irrational beliefs held by many people. Help the students to identify which beliefs they hold. Then have them write down a more functional belief. Encourage them to make signs as reminders which will help them to relearn the more rational belief.

1. It is a necessity for me to be loved and approved of by nearly all significant people in my life.
   CHANGE NEEDED

2. I should be competent and achieving in all respects in order to be a worthwhile person.
   CHANGE NEEDED

3. I should severely blame myself and others for my mistakes and wrongdoings; and by punishing myself or others for errors, I will help prevent future errors.
CHANGE NEEDED

4. It is catastrophic when things do not go just the way I want them to go.
CHANGE NEEDED

5. Unhappiness is caused by factors outside myself and I have little or no ability to control my reactions.
CHANGE NEEDED

6. If I hear of something dangerous or frightening, I should be very concerned and apprehensive that it might occur.
CHANGE NEEDED

7. It is easier for me to avoid many life situations, difficulties and responsibilities than it is to face them.
CHANGE NEEDED

8. I need to be dependent and I need a stronger person than I on whom to rely.
CHANGE NEEDED

9. My past continues to have a very strong effect on my behavior now, just as it always did, and it is almost impossible to overcome.
CHANGE NEEDED

10. I should become upset over other people's problems.
CHANGE NEEDED

11. There is always a perfect solution to every human problem and it is just terrible when I do not find it.
CHANGE NEEDED

The following activities may be done with individuals or with groups:

ACTIVITY 16. TO HELP RELIEVE GUILT (UPPER ELEMENTARY AND SECONDARY)

- Help the student/s to talk to the deceased. "If _____ were here now, what would you say?"
- Have the student/s do something good for someone else.
- Use the group of peers to challenge reasons for irrational guilt.
- Have the student/s write a letter to the deceased.

ACTIVITY 17. TO BUILD SELF-CONCEPT AND EMOTIONAL STRENGTH (UPPER ELEMENTARY AND SECONDARY)

Tree of Life

Have the student/s fill in the components of the tree. (A reproducible tree is provided.) Request that they keep this tree where they will see it frequently: on their mirror at home, in their notebook, on the refrigerator door. The tree will serve as a constant reminder of how rich and strong their lives have been.

Roots: "strengths I've used before"

Branches: "difficult tasks I've mastered"

Knots: "things that get in my way more than they help" (temper, impatience. etc.)

Leaves: "all people important to me now and in my past"

TREE OF LIFE

Directions: In the tree below, write in (and draw in, if necessary):

   Roots: strengths you have used before

 Branches: difficult tasks you have mastered

   Knots: things that get in your way more than they help (example: temper)

  Leaves: all people important to you now and in your past

Put your tree in a place where you will see it frequently!

ACTIVITY 18. TO EXPLORE REACTIONS TO LOSS (SECONDARY)

This exercise can be done as a group activity to build cohesiveness or as an individual activity to allow each child to explore personal perceptions and feelings.

Give the students long strips of paper and have them block off even sections on this strip. Instruct the students to draw in cartoon fashion the sequence of a recent dream. Have each student share the drawing and have them all discuss the feelings they experience when looking at the drawings.

This exercise will help the students both to elicit emotional reactions to the individual real or imagined losses dreamt and to provide validation and comfort from their peers.

ACTIVITY 19. TO HELP STUDENTS EXPLORE SUPPRESSED FEELINGS (SECONDARY)

Help the students to relax; have them close their eyes and request that they use their imaginations.

"Imagine yourself becoming small. You are now four feet, now three feet, now two feet, now one foot. Notice how large the furniture looks, how high a step is. Now continue shrinking until you are absolutely tiny. When you are no more than one-fourth inch, you are going to move inside yourself.

"Standing on your tongue—wet and soft and slipping into your throat—see the inside of the throat and mouth . . . notice the teeth, the darkness, the soft tissue . . . you are going into your body now in search of where you have your feelings stored. You will know when you find it.

"Where are your feelings stored? Behind a wall? In a box? Someplace else? Notice this storage device. What does it feel like? Is it hard, soft, cool, hot? Wht size is it? Does it smell? Does it move?

"Can you lift it? Does it have a cover or door? Can it be opened? If you opened the wall or box or device, what would happen?

"Now ask the storage device why it is holding your feelings? How is it helping you?

"Ask again . . . Are you ready to begin to open the box or wall? Are the feelings ready to come out? It is okay for the feelings to sleep a while longer or you can gradually let them out. It's all okay. Notice how you and your feelings are all okay.

"Now as you are ready, come back to this room and share." When all the students are attentive, discuss their experiences.

ACTIVITY 20. TO HELP STUDENTS WITH AN IDENTIFIED FEAR (SECONDARY)

Have the student relax:

"Close your eyes and think of a very happy time." Allow a few minutes and then calmly walk the student through the situation that is causing the fear. For example, walking past a lot where a murder occurred:

"Imagine yourself on the sidewalk with a friend one block away . . . Relax and breathe deeply and slowly . . . imagine yourself one house away . . . relax, breathing deeply and slowly . . ."

Continue in this manner until the student has, in this imaginative exercise, walked past the lot without anxiety. Replace the example above with whatever fear the student has. Repetition is the key to this exercise—teach the student to practice the relaxing part in reality whenever the empty lot is approached.

ACTIVITY 21. TO BUILD SELF-IMAGE AFTER A LOSS (SECONDARY)

Discussion Questions

Say to the student/s: "It is very important in healing yourself to make some choices about who you are. Crucial events often present the opportunity for questions like these:

1. Do I tend to blame someone else for what's wrong in my life?
2. Do I try to change other people rather than change my own attitudes and actions?
3. Am I willing to assume responsibility for the direction of my own life?
4. Do I live in the present moment or are most of my thoughts about either the past or the future?
5. Do I try to manipulate others into making my decisions for me so that I can blame them if things don't work out?
6. Do I confront the crises of life or do I use alcohol, pills or other escapes to avoid facing them?
7. Do I believe that whatever happens in my life—no matter how painful—I will be given the ability to cope with it?

GROUP ACTIVITIES

You Can Do a Group

If you are one of the many competent counselors who shy away from using groups, you are limiting yourself and the children you serve. When you find yourself consistently choosing individual appointments, it is important to examine the assumptions you are making about yourself and the children. See if you fit any of the following:

I am afraid the group will get out of control. This is perhaps the most common fear. Underlying this fear is the assumption that two or more children may need attention at the same time. This may be true. When this happens:

- address both children by stating an issue common to both
- seat them next to each other and have them talk
- enlist the entire group's help by stating, "Who has something to say to _____ and _____ about _____ ?"

It is my responsibility to help all the children and I am the only one capable of doing that. When counselors are not experienced in groups, this is an easy assumption to make. However, your job as group facilitator is to help students in the group to learn how to help each other. In addition to gaining an understanding and help from others, the children need to learn they can give the same understanding and help to another individual. With even minimal encouragement, group members will help each other. This confirms the old adage, "You teach best what you most need to learn."

I like being needed and depended upon. There is no such thing as a leaderless group and the more communication occurring between people in a group, the more powerful the experience. The counselor is always the leader and as such is needed to perform the magic that happens when people understand each other. The group members still need you to be there just as in one-on-one counseling.

Everyone will be bored and nothing will happen. The very reason children are referred for counseling is because they are not handling some issue in their lives. As group leader, your responsibility is to give direction to the group. With direction, the group provides the perfect opportunity for the students to learn their group responsibilities: sharing, helping, understanding themselves and others, and taking responsibility for their own emotional well-being.

If they are bored, you name the beast by proclaiming, "I'm bored here!" Have them discuss why it is so boring and what would make it less boring.

These are just a few of the assumptions often held by counselors. It is important to identify your assumptions and then get rid of them. Any counselor who can do an effective one-on-one appointment can be a competent group leader as well.

We feel very strongly about the therapeutic value of group work when dealing with issues of loss and trauma. It is truly the treatment of choice for these reasons:

- Loss produces a sense of isolation; groups dispel that sense.
- Shame and self-pity are common bedfellows with depression; in a group where all are experiencing a loss, self-pity is dispelled easily.
- Students seldom absolve their own guilt; forgiveness or permission to forgive oneself comes from others.
- People frequently credit the counselor with "being so understanding, she'll even accept me!" When an entire group accepts the child, the only conclusion that can be reached by the child is, "I'm OK."
- Students see adults as "able to handle anything" and it is easy to see the counselor's strength. It is much more encouraging for students to see the strength in people their own age as they discover how to cope with their tragedies.

With the structured exercise, the conceptual information you have read, and the experience you bring to your work, you will have all the tools you need to activate good groups. You must care or you wouldn't be concerned. That caring will come through and carry you through your beginning stages until you learn to trust yourself.

Conducting a Grief Support Group

1. Meet with the students individually. Have pre-group individualized sessions to establish the need for a group and how to benefit from one. Establish a rapport to ease misconceptions and fears. Encourage participation in the group.

2. Establish the size of the group. Five-member groups are the most harmonious, problem-solving groups. An acceptable size would be four to eight students. As the group increases in size, less time is available for individual problem solving.

3. Decide if it is a continuous or closed group. The continuous group allows students to join at almost any stage. The closed group identifies the participants and no others are allowed to join until a new group is formed.

4. Determine the physical setting. The room selected should have privacy and freedom from noise. A circular seating arrangement provides more eye-to-eye contact and observable, non-verbal responses. It also tends to create a less threatening atmosphere for the student.

5. Set the duration and frequency of the meetings. The leader would need to consider the composition of the group, the needs of the individuals within the group, and limitations within the school. The recommended duration for junior and senior high sessions is approximately one hour. The counseling group should meet at least once a week and, if practical, twice a week.

6. Decide when to terminate the group. The leader *and* the majority of the group decide when they have reached a satisfactory level of coping and if they are ready to terminate the group.

First Group Meeting: A Typical Plan

1. Give an introductory statement about the purpose of the group.
2. Help the group to establish ground rules.
3. After the group has stated its wishes, add your own if not already addressed. Some important factors are:
   • confidentiality
   • honesty
   • nonjudgmental acceptance of others
   • discouragement of tardiness and irregular attendance
4. Inform the participants that they have the option of not participating in an activity if they feel uncomfortable.
5. Do a get-acquainted activity:

Elementary school level—ask each child to introduce himself and declare what animal he would be, if he could be, and why. (Animal can be substituted for by toy, cartoon, movie character, etc.)

Secondary school level—"Each of you is a news reporter. The first thing I will ask you to do is choose a person you do not know. Speak to that person for two minutes and find out something that person has done or a challenging experience that person has had. Then we will pass the microphone (real or imaginary) around and you will be the reporter interviewing your partner for the group."

ACTIVITY 22. GROUP DISCUSSION QUESTIONS ABOUT DEATH (ALL AGES, AS INDICATED)

Discussion Questions for Preschool/Kindergarten

- What happens when a person dies?
- Who knows what a funeral is?
- What do people do at a funeral?
- When a person dies, do you get to see him or her again?
- Can dead people hear you talk to them?

Discussion Questions for 6–8 Year Olds

- What happens when a person dies?
- Do you think a dead person gets cold in the ground?
- Where do they go?
- Do they come back?
- Is death a punishment? For whom?
- If a person wishes someone dead, can that really happen?

Discussion Questions for 9–11 Year Olds

- What happens when a person dies?
- Why do you think young people sometimes die?
- What do you think a person who has died needs?
- When a person dies, do you ever get to see him or her?
- When a person has someone they love die, what do you think is hardest for that person?
- What helps someone recover from the death of someone they love?

Discussion Questions for Teenagers

- How do you think you would react if a classmate of yours died?
- How about other reactions some students may have?
- What do you believe happens to a person after death?
- Why do you think people have difficulty talking about death?
- The question of "What does it all mean?" comes to mind, especially when a young person dies. How do we find that meaning?

ACTIVITY 23. TO HELP CLASSMATES EXPRESS COMPASSION (ALL AGES, FOR A GROUP OR A CLASS)

When a loss occurs in the life of a student or faculty member, these guidelines may be followed. They will serve both as a tool to help the children respond to their classmate as well as a preventive tool to identify other children who may be hurting

Contact the child:

If teacher-referred:

- inform parents
- report back to the teacher, indicating how he/she can help

If parent-referred:

- inform the teacher
- report to the parent/s and the teacher, indicating how they can help

If the child is self-referred:

- discuss with the child and report to teachers and parent/s

Speak with the class or peer group (when the child is not there):

- Discuss what the student may be feeling.
- Discuss how they can help their fellow student.

- Ask if others have had similar losses. This questioning may determine if help is needed by others and will help the children relate to the student and one another.
- Have the class do something for the classmate. An example would be to make cards.

ACTIVITY 24. PROVIDING CLASSROOM GUIDANCE FOR A LOSS (PRIMARY)

(This exercise will help children gain an understanding of emotions associated with loss.)

Bring stickers, candy, inexpensive toy gadgets, and blackboard chalk.

Allow each child to take a sticker, candy or a toy, and then talk about the reason for choosing that object. (In a large group, have each tell a partner and have a few share their views with the group.)

Appoint two children to take the items away from their classmates.

Then ask for the children's reactions and add observations yourself—for example, "Suzie, you were smiling before; now you're not." or ask questions, like "Did anyone get angry?"

Tell them they can now have their stickers, candy, or toy back and this time they can keep them. Exploring their feelings helps them identify feelings and thoughts attached to a loss.

To continue the program, put this face on a flipchart:

Ask:

What face is this?

Can you remember a time when you were sad?

What helped you the most?

What did your friends say to you?

Now put this face on the flipchart:

Ask:

What face is this?

Can you remember a time when you were angry because someone left you?

Now there is another face I'd like to show you but I cannot draw it because when children feel this way, they try to hide it. The feeling is guilty. Can you explain what guilty is? Many children feel guilty when someone leaves them. Many children think, If I was a good child, Daddy would have stayed. If I behave and get good grades, maybe he'll come back.

Some children think, Sometimes I'm so mad, I wish they'd die or go away *and if the person really does leave, the child may feel that he or she made it happen.*

Can you remember a time when you wanted Mom and Dad to do something and you did not get what you wanted? How hard did you cry? And you still did not get what you wished for? Lots of things happen and we cannot stop them happening.

If you feel the different ways I described to you, you may want to speak to me again. Talking to someone who understands makes you feel better and I want all of you to feel the best you can.

ACTIVITY 25. TO INTRODUCE A CLASS TO LOSS AND NORMAL REACTIONS TO LOSS (MIDDLE GRADES)

Alerting children before a loss occurs helps them build coping skills to use in times of crisis.

What Is Grief?

We're here to talk about GRIEF. (Write it on the board.)

What do you think of when you hear that word?

Some of you may not think of anything at all; some of you may think of someone who has died because when we think of grief, we think of death.

There are other examples of grief, too:

- *pain over the death of a dog or moving away and leaving your friends*
- *parents separated or divorced*
- *the feeling of rejection when changing teachers or classrooms*
- *failing at something you tried.*

How many of you think you have experienced grief?

We grieve when we have experienced a loss. Do you have any other types of losses?

Grief and Emotions

Grief is really a lot of different emotions that we feel when we have had a loss. List feelings

Why do we feel angry? It just doesn't seem fair!

Why do we feel guilty? It feels like it may be your fault, though it rarely is.

Why do you think you may be confused? Because a loss that is unexpected puts us in the state of shock. It doesn't seem possible that this is really happening to you. That makes it difficult to concentrate.

We all know that it is normal to feel unhappy and sad but does anyone know how long a time most people still feel unhappy? How long did you feel unhappy after you had a big loss?

Why do you think we also are afraid? Perhaps that something might happen to you? Or perhaps you are afraid no one will be there to care for you? Or perhaps you are afraid to get close to anybody again?

A Special Person

Think of a special person you would go to talk to about the way you are feeling. We all need someone special we can talk to. (Discuss with them their special people.)

Completing the Handout

Have the students complete the grief and loss analysis and discuss it with those who are willing to share:

- "Were you surprised by your answers?"

- "What helped you the most?"
- "What things did people say or do that hurt?"

General Comments

"Usually, when you experience a loss, not only are you grieving and hurting, but so is the rest of your family. Sometimes it is hard for them to be there for you because they are hurting. Therefore it is important that you know there are people in your school who are willing to help you."

"It really helps to know that there are people in your classrooms who have felt the same way you do when experiencing a loss."

Name _____ Date _____

LOSS QUESTIONNAIRE

---

1. Identify a loss in your life.

2. How did you feel afterwards? (check one)
   ☐ Angry   ☐ Okay
   ☐ Frightened   ☐ Shocked
   ☐ Guilty   ☐ Sad
   ☐ Confused

3. What helped you feel better?

4. What did people say or do that hurt or did not help?

5. To whom did you turn?

6. Would you like to talk to someone about this now?

ACTIVITY 26. TO DISCUSS THE EFFECTS OF GRIEF (SECONDARY) GROUP OR CLASS)

Begin with Questions:

- How many of you have had someone break up with you? (*loss*)
- How many of you ever changed schools? (*loss*)
- How many of you ever lost a friend? (*loss*)
- How many of you ever experienced a death or a divorce in your family? (*a significant loss*)

Then Explain:

When a loss occurs, even an anticipated loss, people grieve. The only difference is that the intensity of the loss increases the intensity of the grief. Let's take a few minutes now to fill out a loss and grief analysis and discover how you react to a loss.

Discussion with Students:

- What was your most startling discovery?
- What bothered you most?
- Did any questions make you angry? Sad?
- To what did you have the strongest reaction?

Describe the Stages of Bereavement:

As we talk about the stages of grief, remember that anyone of us may go through these stages, even skipping some, overlapping some and returning to others. The important thing I want you to remember is that these emotions are normal and do not indicate "craziness" or "not handling it well." Because you're depressed and not thinking clearly about moving away from friends in another state is no indication you've "lost" it.

Shock or disbelief

- it's a bad movie, not my life
- life seems like a dream, not reality
- they are really coming back
- (divorce) I know Mom and Dad will reunite
- numb feelings

LOSS AND GRIEF ANALYSIS

Think for a moment of a loss you have had. Describe what happened.

What emotional reactions did you have?

What physical reactions did you have?

What helped you to recover?

What hurt more than helped?

How has your life changed because of this loss?

How was how you dealt with this loss similar to the way you deal with other losses?

These thoughts and feelings are normal. Disbelief cushions the emotions from too much information too soon. It's our way of making sure we are not overwhelmed.

Fear

We all operate under the assumption that the world is predictable and we are in control. When a loss occurs, we find we are not in control—we feel fear.

You all know at your age it would be difficult to survive in the world alone. If loss hits your family, you're afraid of what will happen. Who will support me? Will I have to be responsible for my parent? What can you do? Ask questions to find answers you need. Talk to someone.

Anger

Anger is another emotion people feel

- just when I get my life together, this has to happen
- it's not fair

What can you do? Look for constructive ways to let it out. Any suggestions? (write on board)

- create art
- knead bread
- dance to loud music
- build something involving hammering
- chop wood
- sing
- wrestle
- do physical exercise (tennis, running, swimming, etc.)
- challenge yourself physically (football, leg and arm wrestling, etc.)

Depression

Depression shows itself in two ways during teenage years. One we easily recognize, one less so.

First—depression as lethargy:

- over/under eating
- inability to concentrate
- self-deprecation (explain)
- thoughts of suicide
- withdrawal from friends/activities

Second—depression as activity:

- constant partying
- hyperactivity
- overindulgence in chemical use
- self-destructive behavior
- sexual promiscuity
- "running away" in general

Most important to remember:

- "This too shall pass!"
- It is normal.
- It happens so the emotions can heal.

You do not need to keep pace but you do need to keep moving:

- if withdrawing, go out once in a while even if you do not feel like it
- force yourself to do physical exercise/release
- get more sleep and better nutrition because your immune system is weak now

Acceptance

This is when you at last feel comfortable. You begin enjoying people and activities again.

Wrapping it Up:

I know many of you have experienced losses, some more difficult than others. When you are going through the stages of grief, it is helpful to know:

- you are not alone
- some of your questions can be answered
- the pain can be eased
- you are not going crazy

I am your grief counselor and this is how you can contact me . . . (Explain the procedure in your school.)

ACTIVITY 27. TO HELP STUDENTS DEAL WITH ANGER (UPPER ELEMENTARY/SECONDARY)

What Do You Usually Do When You Are Angry?

- have students describe their methods (reinforce good methods immediately, ignore others)
- list all of them on the board as they speak
- have the students categorize their responses into constructive and destructive methods

Which Ones Will Help and Which Ones Could Get You in Trouble?

- help students identify if they fit into the physical, sedentary, creative, or verbal ways of expressing anger
- expand the students' repertoire of skills by asking, "For those of you who prefer a *physical* response, what else can you do? (*creative? verbal?*)

Keep the session lively and fast-paced.

ACTIVITY 28. TO PROMOTE POSITIVE SELF-CONCEPT AFTER A LOSS (SECONDARY)

Making a Crest

Discuss with students: "Many years ago, families who had accomplished something well would record the accomplishment with symbols on a piece of wood or metal. The family would then adopt it as their badge or *crest* and it was a sign to the world of what they could do best. It also served as a reminder of the strength and ability of that family. Families no longer do this but we are going to make an individual crest."

Instructions

1. Cut a large piece of cardboard from a poster or a box in the shape of a crest (any shape crest they choose).
2. Glue white paper on the surface.
3. List the answers to the following questions on a separate sheet of paper:
   - What is the most important event in your life so far?
   - What is your greatest achievement?
   - What are you good at?
   - What are you striving to become?
   - Name something you did well this month.
   - What are you most proud of?
4. Decide on a symbol to represent each accomplishment, and either draw these symbols on your crest or make a collage of collected symbols and paste them on your crest.

Over the next few weeks, have students show their crests to one another and talk about their accomplishments as represented on the crest. This exercise will (1) remind the students of the abilities and strengths they have already used in their lives; (2) give them a sense of self-worth; and (3) bond them in common ideas and competencies they may not have known about before.

ACTIVITY 29. TO INTEGRATE A LOSS OR TRAUMATIC EVENT (ALL AGES)

Group Project

As a group organize or build a project documenting the event or issues around the event:

- build or design a memorial
- begin a SADD chapter in your school
- decorate the trophy cabinet
- begin a class scrapbook
- build a replica of the crisis

- offer assistance to others as a class project: food collection, rebuilding a house, assisting younger people
- place commentary in the newspaper
- write a group story

These shared activities establish the cohesiveness that diminishes the fear and restores the sense of being in control after a traumatic event.

ACTIVITY 30. TO INTEGRATE A TRAGEDY IN A POSITIVE WAY (ALL AGES)

Group Mural or Collage

Have the students in a group depict the common tragic event they shared. Each person's idea for inclusion in the picture must be drawn by that person. Allow the group to reach a consensus about what should be in the mural. (The key to reaching a consensus is to make the mural very large.) When finished, hang the mural in the classroom for awhile and do not take it down until discussion is held about removing it. This gives the students a way to render the incident tangible and integrate it into their lives.

ACTIVITY 31. TO HELP REGAIN A SENSE OF TRUST IN THE WORLD (SECONDARY)

Developing a Disaster Plan

Have the students break into groups of five or six. Each group is to develop a disaster plan.

First, the group must develop ideas to help prevent future incidents of the type that just occurred.

Second, if a similar incident did occur, what would the group plan to handle the aftermath?

Have the students discuss each group's plan and, as a class, decide which ideas they can act on.

Identify the steps needed to follow through on their plans.

This exercise works best if it is an ongoing activity, with attention paid to the activity each day to ensure action. It is the action that restores the sense of control and security in the students. This also builds self-worth and group cohesiveness.

ACTIVITY 32. TO PROMOTE CONFLICT RESOLUTION (SECONDARY)

Mini Lecture on Conflict Resolution

We usually learn how to handle conflict from family members. What does your family do when conflict arises? (Have students discuss different ways.) The ways people handle conflict fall into different patterns such as:

Avoidance some people attempt to avoid conflict situations or certain types of conflict. These people tend to repress emotional reactions, look the other way, or leave the situation entirely (for example, quit a job, leave school, get divorced). Either they cannot face up to such situations effectively or they do not have the skills to negotiate them satisfactorily.

Although avoidance strategies do have survival value in those instances where escape is possible, they usually do not provide the individual with a high level of satisfaction. The avoiding person is left wondering about his/her own courage and persistence and has doubts and fears about meeting the same type of situation in the future.

Defusion This tactic is essentially a delaying action used to cool off the situation, at least temporarily, or to keep the issues so unclear that attempts at confrontation are improbable. Some examples of defusion are: resolving minor points while avoiding or delaying discussion of the major problem, postponing a confrontation until a more favorable time, and avoiding clarification of the real issues underlying the conflict. Again, as with avoidance strategies, such tactics work when delay is possible but they typically result in feelings of dissatisfaction, anxiety about the future and concerns about oneself.

Confrontation The third major strategy involves an actual confrontation of conflicting issues or persons. Confrontation can be subdivided further into POWER strategies and NEGOTIATION strategies.

Power strategies include the use of physical force (fighting, war), bribery (money or favors), and punishment (withholding love or money, extortion). Such tactics are effective for one (he wins, the other loses). Unfortunately, however, for the loser the real conflict has just begun. Hostility, anxiety, and actual physical damage are the byproducts of these power tactics. More and more time is spent in thinking of ways to get even and eventually the brooding loser of this conflict will lash out with power and then both sides are hurt.

Negotiation strategies allow both sides to win. The aim of negotiation is to resolve the conflict with a compromise or a solution which is satisfying to both parties involved in the conflict. Negotiation, then, seems to provide the most positive and the least negative byproduct of all conflict resolution strategies.

Conflict Management: A Self-Examination

The participants are asked to join you , the facilitator, in a visualization designed to help them examine their individual conflict-resolution strategies. For approximately ten minutes, you will guide the group through the following fantasy. Feel free to embellish the fantasy to fit the group.

Ask the students to get comfortabl, close their eyes, and think about the present moment, the sounds around them, the temperature of the room, and where they are sitting. Then again request them to relax, and say:

"Using your imagination, I am going to help you develop mental pictures. Imagine yourself walking down a street (or hallway or path) and begin to see in the distance a familiar person. Suddenly you recognize that it is the person with whom you are most in conflict. You realize you must decide quickly how to deal with this person. As that person comes closer, a number of alternatives flash through your mind."

"Decide right now what you will do."

"As the person approaches do what you have imagined and notice the results."

"The person is gone now. How do you feel? How does the other person feel? What is that person likely to do now?"

"Open your eyes when you are ready."

After the students emerge from their fantasies, have them spend five minutes writing:

1. the alternative ways of acting that they considered.
2. the one they chose to act upon.
3. the outcome of their action, their feelings and their opponent's reaction.

Split the group into smaller groups of three. Have each student share the chosen way of acting and the results. Each group should have one volunteer to record the different ways chosen by that particular group. Then have these small groups brainstorm alternative ways of dealing with the situation.

When the whole group reconvenes, share all the alternatives generated and list on the board.

Lead a discussion on the level of satisfaction (short-term and long-term), the results, the feelings.

Variations:

1. A participant can volunteer his/her visualization to be role-played in front of the entire group. Role-players can be coached by subgroups. Then the persons discuss how they felt from the experience.

2. Role-playing can be done in threes, with one member being an observer, the other being the confronter, the third being the confrontee. Switch roles.

3. This same format can be used in small groups with real-life conflict between two group members. Use the rest of the group to coach each person in learning negotiation.

PART V

SPECIAL CONCERNS FOR SPECIFIC CRISIS

Introduction

IN THIS SECTION, you will learn about some aspects of a crisis that can give it a more serious, widespread effect on a school and community. Then you will learn about four special kinds of crisis—suicide, violence, natural disasters, and the dying child in a classroom—and ways to either prevent them or deal with them more effectively.

FACTORS THAT INCREASE THE LIKELIHOOD OF TRAUMA

The National Organization for Victim Assistance has identified certain types of incidents which affect how widespread the effects of a tragedy will be.

Incidents within Closely Knit Communities

Many elementary schools draw from neighborhoods with children and families who have grown up together. Because of this, an event occurring even in the personal lives of one of the students could affect the lives of many children. In one case, when the mother of a kindergarten boy committed suicide, the administration realized it had to become involved because many of the children were distraught. The children all came from a subdivision having many interdependent families. Rumors were rampant. The deceased mother's depression had been the subject of concern among many neighbors. The families often spent their holidays together and frequently exchanged babysitting. Prior to coming to school that morning, many children had overheard their parents' comments about the death. Although the school ordinarily would not have involved itself so thoroughly in addressing the issue, circumstances in this case demanded a response.

The school was asked not to reveal the fact that the death was caused by suicide. In the classrooms, the teachers helped the students understand how to respond to the boy when he returned to school. They helped the children understand that this death did not mean their own mothers were at risk of dying. When questions about the cause of death arose, the teachers said they did not know. The students asking this question were spoken to individually by the counselors or teachers. These children were encouraged to speak with their parents about the rumors they had heard. The school also convened parents' group to inform those parents whose children were asking questions. Parents who were calling the school for information on handling their child were also invited. Because of the responsive and thorough action taken by the school administration, a crisis was readily resolved before getting out of control.

In addition to the school community affected, there are the mini-communities—the scout troop, church youth organizations, and various community-sponsored sports teams. When a child belongs to such a community group, the circle of influence is considerably broadened. The death of a sixth-grader who plays in a Pop Warner football league may affect children in several grades and several schools. Those schools must be prepared to deal with the loss.

Incidents with Multiple Eye Witnesses

Although it is traumatic for a student to hear of a classmate who has been killed, actually witnessing the accident has a more extensive effect. The intense emotional reaction in the children who have seen an accident will fuel the emotional reactions of other students, thereby making the total impact more serious and widespread.

One such incident occurred when a 13-year-old student stepped off a school bus and was struck by a hit-and-run driver. The children he rode with daily viewed the tragedy from the bus and reacted with much greater intensity than if they had only heard about the accident. Several ran away from the school bus while others began to tear at its interior. Several stood frozen in silent panic. In the aftermath of this incident those students were plagued with nightmares and fears.

When the Victims Have a Special Significance

The Challenger Space Shuttle disaster is an example of one individual victim possessing exceptional significance for the community. All the astronauts were important, but it was the teacher on board, Christa McCauliffe, who was chosen to represent the leaders of our youth. She became a symbol of the ordinary, respected member in any community, the everyday American accepting the challenges of life. As such, many of us identified with her. For a few moments we could vicariously experience the feeling that something as wondrous as space travel was for all of us. When the explosion occurred, we felt the horror of the catastrophe and were intimately affected by it because of our close identification to one of those on board.

When a Community Is Exposed to Carnage or Misery

The desecration of human life that occurs in certain tragedies, explosions, wild random shootings, fatal fires and certain natural disasters profoundly affects even the most hardened individuals. When the aftermath of the tragedy results in extensive and prolonged rescue operations being observed by many spectators, the trauma is heightened by the length of time it takes before anyone truly knows who is safe and alive and who is not.

Incidents that Call for Numerous Rescue Workers

In Bronson, Florida, an accident occurred and children were trapped inside their school bus. Many businessmen witnessed the accident and began the rescue of the youngsters before the emergency personnel arrived at the location. Because the community was small and had few outside resources to draw upon, the school provided not only information but also discussions and group meetings for the townspeople affected by these deaths. The school thereby fulfilled its responsibility of assisting the people involved in the rescue operations.

Incidents that Attract a Great Deal of Media Attention

By bringing news stories into our homes each evening, the media bring into our lives those incidents which people ordinarily hold remote. In 1987, after the *USS Starke* was attacked in the Persian Gulf, the schools in Mayport, Florida, homeport of the destroyer, were under siege from the press seeking news about the reactions. The national news made those who died more real to us and more people were drawn into the mourning. When the local elementary school held its memorial service it was attended by over four-hundred citizens. The school had not anticipated how important the service they were conducting for their students would be for the entire community.

SUICIDE PREVENTION

Suicide is not triggered by the mere mention of the word and preparation for a suicide crisis does not denote the expectation of a suicide. Planning is an insurance policy aimed at eliminating suicide when possible and minimizing its devastating consequences.

When a suicide occurs, faculty and students are emotionally shaken to the core. It is then that a familiar, practiced plan provides a crutch for all to depend on. In the midst of a tragedy, many small decisions must be made and by careful preplanning, the principal is assured that any decisions made by the staff will reflect a cohesive approach and consistent action.

A thorough plan includes three levels:

Prevention A school-wide program to reduce the probability of a student choosing suicide as an option for coping.

Intervention An effective counseling and referral system to help students at risk.

Postvention A plan of action to reduce the possibility of a suicide cluster after a suicide has occurred.

Suicide Risk Factors

Students most at risk of attempting suicide and of behavioral problems in general tend to exhibit one or more of the following characteristics:

- a sense of not belonging in a school
- a sense of having a restricted future because of doing poorly in school
- alienation from peers
- low level of family support

In addition to these personal risk factors, there are certain environmental factors in the school that increase the risk of suicide:

- recent transitions imposed by the system
- lack of specialized programs
- a social climate with strong cliques and factions
- alienation and rejection of certain students
- too much attention given to suicide threats or attempts

An attentive response to a suicide attempt can be overwhelmingly attractive to a student who feels lonely or distressed and seeks seemingly unattainable acceptance. Responding professionals must take the threat seriously and demonstrate sincere concern, but should downplay involvement of the student body and prevent any glorification of the attempt.

Prevention: What Works?

There is a lack of empirical evidence to support how well traditional suicide prevention programs work. For instance, preliminary findings by Dr. David Shaffer suggest that a large number of cases do not fit the widely-taught "early warning signs" (Shaffer, 1989). Because of this uncertainty, and because there has been documentation of an increase in suicides during a period immediately following a television drama about suicide (Phillips, 1979; Gould & Shaffer, 1986), we believe that suicide prevention programs should take a broad-brush approach. Rather than teaching students about suicide specifically, a program should seek to:

- help teachers and counselors identify the broad spectrum of "at risk" students
- ensure that school personnel such as counselors will be available to help identified students (rather than tied up with tasks such as scheduling students, as frequently occurs at the secondary level)
- diminish the predisposing conditions of the school community
- increase the coping skills of the students.

Students themselves appear to prefer this approach. Recommendations they have given to Iris Bolton, Director of the Link Counseling Center in Atlanta, include:

- increasing student acceptance of counseling through attitude change
- increasing students' ability to cope
- providing peer counseling
- providing wallet cards that list coping skills and hot lines for help
- providing more help for coping with depression
- offering drama classes that focus on common teen problems.

Components of a Comprehensive Program

The following guidelines are a synthesis of recommendations made by researchers Dr. Cleve Hollar (1987), Dr. Barry Garfinkel (1989), Dr. David Shaffer (1989) and Dr. Veronica Vieland (1989), who together represent a spectrum of educational and psychiatric perspectives. Each component will be described in detail in the pages that follow.

A COMPREHENSIVE SUICIDE PREVENTION PROGRAM

Training for Educators

- Identification and referral of high-risk youth
- Positive emotional development

Curriculum Guide for Students (all levels)

- Coping skills
- Identification of depression
- Coping with depression
- Problem-solving techniques
- Decision-making strategies
- Stress management

Evaluation of Troubled Youth

Follow-Up of Community Referrals and Internal Contacts

Postvention Planning

Having Consultation Available to Schools Developing Prevention Programs

Evaluation of Program Success

Adequate Funding

Training for Educators

Teachers and counselors, more than any other professionals, are in a unique position to identify troubled children. Most programs to train them in suicide prevention focus on the signs and symptoms of impending suicide, but many teens who have attempted suicide have not followed this pattern. More recent training includes the signs of depression, since depression is the one factor common to all suicide attempts and completions. Depression also precipitates other problematic behavior. This early identification process therefore helps prevent a myriad of troublesome behaviors.

Most suicides occur in response to an actual or perceived loss. Young people have very little experience coping with grief and are often left to deal with it by themselves. Training educators to help and understand children who are grieving is an effective suicide-prevention tool. In Duval County (Florida) Public Schools, a grief counseling program in operation for several years found that 65 percent of the students the guidance counselors normally saw had loss issues as the basis for the behavior or problems for which they were referred. In another study analyzing completed suicide notes, it was determined that 72 percent of the completed suicides were students who, in early childhood, had lost a parent due to death or divorce.

The most widely accepted and least controversial aspects of prevention strategy are: (1) providing education for identification of high risk students, and (2) referral of these students for counseling. Studies have found that teachers trained in suicide prevention regarded suicidal statements as possibly serious instead of "nothing to worry about." These teachers were also more knowledgeable about which students to refer. Although it is not known if these informed responses actually decrease the suicide rate, schools which have extensively used these components report increased referrals of high-risk students to the Guidance Department.

The following inclusions for suicide training are recommended by the *Report of the Secretary Task Force on Youth Suicide:*

- Information on acute and chronic risk factors for youth suicide.
- Information on behavioral manifestations of depression, schizophrenia, and conduct disorders in the school setting.
- Information and sources for referring students at risk.
- Training in communication skills to approach and engage children at risk and their families.
- Developing plans for school systems to respond to a student death or suicide.
- Positive emotional development of youth and the importance of experiences to enhance self-concept.

In addition, Dr. Bryan Tanney (1989) of Calgary General Hospital in Canada has developed the Foundation Workshop, a suicide prevention training course designed for a multi-discipline audience, and the American Association of Suicidology have provided a Suicide Prevention Training Manual that has been used by crisis centers now for almost a decade.

Curriculum Guidelines and Projects for Students

Given the controversy about the effectiveness of suicide-specific information to students, it is recommended that any specific suicide information given to the students be embodied in a course addressing healthful living. The emphasis should be on activities to enhance self-concept and skill-building exercises, including techniques for coping with depression and recognizing the danger signs of suicide. Many school systems have implemented such programs system-wide: examples include the Youth Stress Management Program at Solanco High School in Quarryville, PA, the Student Assistance in Life Program (SAIL); and Quest Program supported by the Lions' Club of America.

Evaluation of Troubled Youth

Identification of the high-risk student by the teacher is only the first step in prevention. School counselors must be trained to assess and speak confidently with a suicidal student. They must also have an attitude of respect for the student and composure with the issue of suicide. And it is absolutely essential that enough time, free from scheduling, be allotted to ensure counselor competency. This constitutes the first step of the evaluation process.

The issue of confidentiality surfaces when addressing suicide. Although confidentiality is critical for most areas of concern with our youth, the one time to break it is with a potential suicide. The student should be told by the counselor that confidentiality will be broken because of concern for the student's well-being. The parents must be notified along with the professional to whom the referral is made.

Following up on Referrals

The referral of a troubled child to a community resource often ends up with very little follow-up. One of the finest models working to ensure that high-risk students are not forgotten is the Care Team of Duval County Schools in Florida. It is a team composed of five members who respond to calls from guidance counselors when the problem is beyond their expertise. (The Care Team also mans a 24-hour hot line for troubled teens to call.) These highly-trained counselors provide more in-depth therapy than the Guidance Office has the time or expertise to provide. They operate within the school system, circumventing the problem of the child not reaching the community referral sources. If after several weeks of intervention the student is still in need of counseling, the team is well-established with community resources so that follow-through is highly assured. Because the Care Team is part of the school system, members are also in a position to make recommendations to the schools on behalf of the student in need.

Postvention Planning

There is no disagreement among the experts in the field of suicidology that postvention activities must take place in the event of a suicide. A vital component of any prevention program is to have a postvention plan in place prior to any incident occurring in your school. This topic is addressed in detail in Part IV since these activities also constitute the aftermath of the crisis plan introduced to you in this book.

Consultation

Consultation for a school or a system planning a prevention program is usually available from state departments of education. When that is not possible, you can consult materials published by the American Association of Suicidology, the Center for Disease Control, the Samaritans, or the New Jersey Department of Human Services. A complete list of these and other sources and their addresses follows this section.

Evaluation of Prevention Programs

Although suicidal prevention programs have proliferated in the country, no hard data is available at this time to validate any of them. Private interest groups, mental health agencies, and educational systems have spawned numerous "suicide prevention projects" without knowledge of their effectiveness. Organizations dealing with the problems of suicide threats and completions seek concise, timely, and practical solutions, while researchers focus on the validity of their attempts at solutions. As a result, there is a lack of communication and an element of resistance to evaluation and recommendations.

The consequences are quite serious: consider the unsettled controversy about whether suicide prevention should be approached through suicide-specific information disseminated to a broad population of students or if it should be packaged in a general mental health model without the issue of suicide becoming a focal point. Without this kind of knowledge, it is possible we encourage the very behavior we are working so hard to discourage.

At this point, unfortunately, criteria to assess these programs have not been established. Doing so has become a major priority for research funding with the National Institute of Mental Health.

Adequate Funding

The need for adequate funding for effective suicide prevention programs and the research to evaluate them is self-evident. That does not mean that much funding is available. Ideally, the federal government provides states, schools, or nonprofit organizations with funds through grants. State legislatures that mandate suicide prevention programs often fund them, but not all do, Florida being a case in point. In seeking funds for a comprehensive program, check out federal, state and private sources, but realize that local funding may be your only source.

Additional Activities and Programs

The Secretary's Task Force also recommends creating additional programs in the community and the schools to help with social problems inherent in the populations that constitute potential suicide victims. They recommend having:

- A range of primary prevention programs based on the Head Start Model and aimed at disadvantaged youths.
- Programs that integrate troubled youth into a social network.
- Programs aimed at troubled youth who fall outside the range of traditional programs, or those with multiple high-risk factors.

SUICIDE POSTVENTION

Postvention, which refers to the actions taken following a suicide, is also an inherent part of prevention, because the potential risk of suicide exists for those people directly and even remotely affected by a suicidal death. The Center for Disease Control reports that most suicide clusters occur among adolescents and clusters account for 1–5 percent of completed suicides. There are no accurate statistics on the number of suicide attempts made in reaction to a suicide among teenagers but we do know there is great potential for a single suicide in a school to trigger suicide clusters. Therefore, it is essential that the aftermath of a suicide be handled immediately with expertise and understanding.

In such an aftermath, the school collectively becomes a suicide survivor and, in that respect, is subject to all the emotions of any individual survivor: guilt, anger, anxiety and denial. Anxiety is especially rampant after a young person commits suicide; all the intense emotional reactions are amplified by having so many people in one place who are survivors.

As survivors themselves, the administrators of the school will experience intense personal reactions while they are also being affected by the emotional response of the other survivors. Principals, in particular, tend to feel paternal or maternal toward their staff and students. For them, the sense of responsibility for students does not end with the bell at three o'clock when the students leave. Because they are emotionally affected at the time of a suicide, a plan of positive action should be in place *beforehand.*

The intervention-response must be in place and ready to go immediately to prevent many long-term disasters. In one junior high scool, when a student committed suicide, the administration sought to deny any reactions or their need to be involved since the suicide occurred at the boy's home. Junior high students are not known for their ability to control their feelings and within two days the emotion-charged environment became disruptive: many students misbehaved, others were absent from school (with and without parental permission), and teachers responded with great anxiety both to the censorship of the topic and to the disruption by the students. Three days later, the parents began to blame the school for the student's suicide. Under pressure from the school board and the faculty, the principal called in additional counselors from the community and other schools. The students and the faculty required extended support for several months after the incident occurred. Much time could have been saved had the counseling begun immediately while the reactions were more controllable. In a school full of teenagers, quick action can mean the difference between pandemonium and regulated orderliness.

A Community Problem

The prevention of cluster suicides is a community problem and the community as a whole should be involved in this task. Because the schools are considered the guardians of our children, however, community action groups must often be hosted by the school system.

Developing a Community Crisis Response Plan

Whether the school system is the host agency or just the impetus behind the community action, it must be a leader in developing the plan. The format for developing a community committee is similar to that for creating an in-house crisis team (which is addressed in part I and Part II of this book).

Representatives on the committee should include:

- educators
- public health personnel
- mental health personnel

- suicide crisis centers' personnel
- youth leaders (churches, scouts, athletic teams)
- local government officials

The host agency orchestrates the committee. It is critical that the various representatives reach a committee consensus about the plan so that its implementation in the wake of a suicide goes smoothly. In the absence of crisis, it becomes the duty of the host agency to keep the plan alive, once it has been developed, by periodically calling the committee together to discuss maintenance or revisions. For instance, has the Emergency Room staff at the local hospital changed? Does the local newspaper have a new editor? Has the community opened a new school? To maintain the plan, education and revisions must occur when changes in the community take place. An outdated plan is as effective as no plan at all.

Community-Wide Reporting

Another significant duty of the committee is to develop a community-wide reporting system. An effective communication network will not only alert relevant community personnel in the event of a suicide but will also help to thwart further suicide attempts. When little communication exists between community resources, a suicide cluster could be well underway before the pattern is recognized. The following scenario is possible: a teenager commits suicide and both the police and school know about it. Within days, another teenager attempts suicide. This time, the Emergency Room knows, but since the youth is a drop-out, the school is not alerted. The next day another troubled teen speaks to his probation officer about suicide and is referred to a mental health agency. These teenagers may have known one another and could be influencing each other's actions. Without an established communication structure, the community committee will have no idea that a cluster is beginning.

The relevant resources to be included in the reporting of an adolescent suicide AND attempts are:

- hospitals and emergency room personnel
- emergency services and rescue personnel
- academic resources
- clergy
- PTA and other parent groups
- suicide crisis centers
- survivor groups

- police
- media
- committee members
- educators (Superintendent, student services director, and principals, especially for junior high and high schools.)

What to Tell Community Resources

When meeting with or assembling the community resources, there are several tasks which you must perform:

1. Educate all of them about the plan. Include the responsibilities of each representative group if a suicide cluster should begin.
2. Enlist their aid in monitoring all attempts made.
3. Cross-train groups to know how to handle their area of responsibility regarding (a) reporting, (b) providing services, and (c) knowing whom to contact for help.
4. Educate the media about their responsibility in handling news of adolescent suicide.

When to Enact a Community Plan

Parts of the community plan, such as the reporting system, are always enacted regardless of the number of suicides or attempts. Because schools have an agenda that must be adhered to even after the suicide of a student or teacher, the community committee should be involved so that no one agency or the school is considered derelict in its duties. Have the committee answer the questions of the press.

A suicide cluster plan should take place when:

1. Suicides or attempts occur in a shorter time than usual for that community.
2. One or more traumatic deaths occur, especially among teens.

Other Responsibilities of the Community Committee

1. Counseling after a suicide, especially of a young person, should be provided for the community. This is especially true for the rescue personnel involved.

2. Providing information to the community is essential. There is where you use your academic resources to inform parents, in particular, who will be concerned about how to interpret normal teenage erratic behavior and will need the reassurance of professionals that their sons and daughters are normal.

3. Appointing a spokesperson to address the community through the media. Accurate information must be provided without graphic details of how the suicide was committed. For instance, the spokesperson could say the student overdosed on drugs without describing where the body was found, how the drugs were obtained, the dosage, the type of drug or the details of any messages left behind.

Implementing a Suicide Crisis Plan within a School

Identifying High-Risk Students

An essential step in developing your plan is to train teachers, coaches, deans, and counselors to identify high-risk students. In the case of adolescent suicide clusters, these are the people who are considered at risk:

- relatives and close friends of the deceased
- boy/girlfriend of the deceased
- pall bearers at the funeral
- hospital visitors if the deceased had made previous attempts
- students absent in the following week if not clearly for an illness
- people outside of the school having had close involvement with the deceased
- students with a history of depression
- students with weak social supports
- students who recently moved into the school
- students with known family troubles
- anyone involved in past or present suicidal attempts

When these students are identified by the teacher, they should be screened by the guidance counselor or a mental health professional.

Announcing the Death

When planning how to announce a suicide, remember that the emotions aroused by a suicide are more complex than by any other form of death. Containing these intense feelings is imperative for retaining control. With this heightened emotionality will come distortion of the facts: the rumors generated are usually graphic and more gruesome than the actual event.

Teachers do not have ready answers for the questions that come up in response to a suicide. It is essential for the teachers to be told privately and then given time for their reactions to ebb. They must also be given information about where to send students, what to say to students, and the details of the school's plan.

Students who were close to the deceased should be told privately, both for their own well-being and so they do not have to experience the emotional reaction of other students who are less likely to be as upset.

After the teachers and close friends have been informed, the teacher, and counselor should address the classes much in the same manner as any other death is announced.

SAMPLE ANNOUNCEMENTS FOR SUICIDE

If the death has been declared a suicide:

> We are sad to announce that _____ took his life last night. Memorial services will be made by his family. Counseling will be provided for those who wish to speak with a counselor. It is always a shock when we hear of someone taking his or her life. Let's cancel our work today to discuss this.

If the death has not been declared suicide or if that fact has not been made public:

> _____ died last night of a gunshot wound. He apparently had a gun in his hand when it fired. Counseling will be provided for those who wish to speak with someone. When an unexpected incident such as this occurs, it helps to discuss it. Regular classwork will be canceled to allow time for discussion.

Counseling: Get Help

The screening and counseling of high-risk students is very time-consuming and the necessity of immediate attention places excessive demands on most counseling departments. More than likely, the counseling department will not be able to handle the amount of work needed on the first few days after a suicide. Plan for additional help from the community mental health and suicide crisis centers and provide space for them to see students. Community mental health professionals usually respond readily to such emergencies, but prior arrangements should be made. If the resources are not readily available, you may need to contract with a few professionals.

Memorial Services

It is advisable *not* to hold a memorial service in response to a suicide because the service tends to dramatize and glorify the deceased and the suicidal act. The veneration feeds into the magical thinking of teenagers at a time when they are only marginal in their functioning ability. They could easily begin thinking, in response to a memorial service, "Look how many people would miss me if I were gone!" without realizing they would not be around to see who missed them.

Students should be allowed to go to the funeral services provided by the family. This is important for the resolution of their grief. However, there should be no active participation by the school. Staff members should not speak at the funeral, although their attendance alone is not disruptive to the students. The school should continue with its regular class schedule after the initial discussion following the announcement.

Individual or small group sessions with counselors should be unobtrusively provided to serve the students who need to talk. Students will not have their minds entirely on their work and teachers should provide easy assignments, introducing no new material for the remainder of the week. Group commemoratives should be discouraged if they venerate the deceased. If students want to do something positive, their actions should be focused on helping the survivors or promoting healthy living skills.

Addressing the Media

The most sensitive duty a principal has following the suicidal death of a student or teacher is addressing the media. Serious consequences can easily result if this is improperly handled. It is well documented that the media's sensationalizing of adolescent suicide can increase the number of additional suicides within a short period of time.

- When possible, use the community committee spokesperson to address the media. This is not possible, however, if the suicide occurred on school grounds. The principal is then the one to stand before the press. For example, a 16-year-old honor roll student walked out to her car during a class period and shot herself. The shot was heard and several students found the body. The principal had to respond. In another incident, a student drove off a cliff well after school hours. This time, the community spokesperson was able to answer the press. The principal must be prepared, however, to accompany the spokesperson with follow-up remarks if requested.

- Information should be factual and not graphic. Avoid either glorifying or vilifying the deceased. If all the information is not known, hold frequent meetings with the press to update them as facts become available.
- Direct the press to other resources as well. Again, this is where you can use your academic resource to provide information to the community on the topic of adolescent suicide. Referrals could be made to local college professors, mental health clinicians, or the Center for Disease Control in Atlanta.
- Avoid whitewashing. Honest answers do not lead to embarrassing or libelous situations.
- Focus on steps taken, the development of the plan and the resources supporting your action plan.
- Enlist the aid of the media to report how community members may find counseling help. Ask the media to promote the Hot-Line available in your community.
- Remind the media of the consequence of sensationalizing a teenage suicide. Oftentimes reporters simply do not realize the impact their statements may have on other students. (Back yourself up with reliable figures and sources.)

Debriefing

No one involved in the aftermath of a school suicide will remain untouched emotionally. Teachers and staff are no exception and a debriefing for them is imperative. Teachers and counselors may feel tremendous guilt and anger resulting from a sense of responsibility in their relationship with the student who committed suicide or the other students who are functioning poorly as a result of the suicide. They must have an opportunity to discuss these emotions.

The debriefing should be conducted with small groups of people and, preferably, by a community counselor. Directive information given about normal reactions and how to handle them is usually helpful. A few may speak about their feelings and their reactions, but for the most part, the best help is given by informing them. Since they are teachers, the conversation will tend to dwell on preventing adolescent suicide and the stigma of suicide. This is not helpful. What the staff members need most is to focus on their own emotional reaction. Preventive measures can be dealt with later.

Outreach

Programs may need to be provided for the parents and the community. Parents become apprehensive about their own children after an incident takes place in which a child dies. They question their own child-rearing methods, including discipline and involvement with their children. They also question the school's actions with their children. By having a recognized expert addressing these concerns, the school provides reassurance for the parents, exchanges important information, helps some children, and expresses its care, concern and involvement to the community.

Sources of Suicide Prevention Training Information

American Association of Suicidology (1977). *Suicide Prevention Training Manual* (1st. ed.). Merck Sharp & Dohme, West Point, Pa.: American Association of Suicidology, 2459 S. Ash St. Denver, Co. 80222

Center for Disease Control, Division of Injury Epidemiology and Control, Atlanta, Ga. 30333.

National Committee on Youth Suicide Prevention, 666 Fifth Avenue New York, N.Y. 10103

Positive Action, P.O. Box 2347, 321 Eastland Drive, Twin Falls, Idaho, 83303

QUEST Program, Lions' Clubs of America, 6655 Sharonwood Blvd., Columbus, Ohio, 43229.

Ramsey, R., Tanney, B., Tierney, R., Lang, W., (1986), *A Curriculum and Training Program for Suicide Prevention: Help for the Helpers.* Manuscript submitted for publication.

Samaritans, 600 Commonwealth Avenue, Boston, Ma. 02215

Suicide Information and Education Center, 721 14th Street N.W., Calgary, Alberta, Canada T2N 2A4

Youth Stress Management Guidance Program, Solanco High School, 585 Solanco Road, Quarryville, Pa. 17566

Youth Suicide National Center, 1825 I Street N.W., Suite 400, Washington, D.C. 20006

Youth Suicide Prevention: Meeting the Challenge in New Jersey Schools, N.J. Dept. of Human Services, Division of Mental Health and Hospitals, Trenton, N.J., 08625

PREVENTING VIOLENCE IN THE SCHOOL

When we think of school violence, images come to mind of a 14-year-old wielding a weapon in a school hall. Yet these sensationalized acts of violence do not occur in isolation. They are an outgrowth of a complex series of factors which for the most part are identifiable, predictable, and controllable.

Violence in schools is not a new phenomenon. In seventeenth-century France, citizens refrained from walking past schools due to attacks by marauding students. In eighteenth and nineteenth-century England, head-masters were frequently backed up with military assistance. And in 1843, Horace Mann, promotor of public education, commented on American schools being characterized by "idleness and disorder." More recent history has introduced nonscholastic problems for students—substance abuse, suicide, rape, robbery and assault—that are far different from the school memories of most adults. In the forties, major nonscholastic concerns were considered to be running in the halls, talking, making noise, wearing inappropriate clothing, chewing gum, and an occasional scuffle. Rarely do adults today encounter the types of traumas their children face on a daily basis.

Violence and conflict significantly affect the educational process and decrease its effectiveness. Crime and the anticipation of crime reduce teacher and student commitment to education. And it is the uncommitted student who is more likely to use violence in the school, thus perpetuating the problem. Students experiencing victimization or viewing fellow students being victimized have increased anxiety and fear, which decrease their commitment to education. Among teachers, it is the newest and the youngest who are most likely to be victims of school violence.

Community Factors that Promote Violence

Certain elements in the community, the school facility and school programs either passively promote violence or create an environment in which it will occur.

- *Poverty and unemployment* promote significant tension in the family, social unrest in the community, and little hope for progress in the future. This limited hope decreases the relevancy of schoolwork.

- *A transient population* allows only minimal identification with the school and the community making many students wish they were "somewhere else."

• *Pro-violent values*—No community outwardly advocates school violence. Yet a hands-off policy about relationship violence, rewarding and advocating the use of aggression to solve problems, the use of unwarranted "strong-arm" tactics by law enforcement officials, and watching certain TV programs and movies tend to encourage violent behavior.

• *The excusing of violence* if the perpetrator was under the influence of alcohol.

• *Prevailing prejudice* in a community provides the excuse to overlook inconsistent treatment of the citizens of that community.

Of course, some environmental attitudes and problems are more easily remedied than others and the school system is not necessarily in the position to implement needed changes in the community. Your awareness, however, of these adverse community attitudes affords the opportunity for you to increase control and protection within your school.

School Facility Factors that Promote Violence

• *Large schools* diminish the sense of belonging and increase alientation. High-risk students are easily "lost in the crowd." Less opportunity exists for teachers to get to know the students personally and provide positive role models for them

• *Overcrowding,* wherever it occurs, increases aggression among people. Overcrowding imposes limitations at an age when the students are seeking freedom. Impulsive, hormone-driven behavior is at its peak and discretion is at its nadir.

• *Lack of resources,* including both materials and staff, reduces the school's ability to inspire the students academically and impairs the directing of impulsive adolescent behavior into constructive learning experiences.

• *Rapid enrollment growth* places many of the above pressures on a school while it adjusts to the increase in new staff members and new students unfamiliar with policies and rules. Many teenage students "test" their new territory and sometimes their "testing" involves aggression or violence. If the number of staff has not caught up to the number of students, this "testing" behavior will not be contained in its early stages and aggression could escalate.

School Program Factors that Promote Violence

- *Lack of cooperation* between teachers and administrators promotes dissension that is likely to be acted out by the students. Teachers have a difficult time enforcing policies with which they do not agree. Students, sensing this ambivalence in the teachers, are deprived of the firm direction and security that results from teamwork and a certain esprit de corps.

- *Teacher silence*—If teachers fail to report incidents because they fear being labeled incompetent in the classroom, the offenders will not experience the school-wide system of consequences for unacceptable behavior. This lack of action passively condones aggression, which can then escalate to violence.

- *A hierarchical pattern of dominance* leads to victimization when it is used to make demands without explanation and without allowing a voice from those to whom the demands are directed. For example, if an administrator wants to decrease the time allowed for student movement between classes, the advice of students and teachers should be sought, because if the decision is made without their input and the students are tardy because of too little time, anxiety and resentment could result as a direct consequence of that decision.

- *The presence of school security* increases tension. It represents an expectation of the need for strong physical tactics. Although at times such precautions are required, security should be introduced only after carefully considering the impact it will have. When security is needed, incorporating the appropriate person into the curriculum or special programs signifies a role beyond that of security and the position can be viewed more positively.

- *Limited educational options*—Lack of alternative education and career preparation services leaves many students' needs unmet by the educational system. These students tend to become less involved in their school and, as uncommitted students, are most likely to release their tension through escalating aggression.

- *Staff attitudes and application of policy* also reinforce violence. Any inconsistency or lack of firmness in the way rules are enforced will be instantly perceived and disliked by the students. The general malaise exhibited by any students or staff who are disengaged from the learning process will promote disharmony and dissension. A lowering of school and staff morale will result if the problem is not resolved promptly.

FACTORS THAT PROMOTE VIOLENCE

Community Factors

- Poverty and unemployment
- Transient population
- Pro-violent values
- Excusing violence under intoxication
- Prevailing community prejudice

School Facility Factors

- Large schools
- Overcrowded school
- Lack of resources (material and personnel)
- Rapid enrollment growth

School Program Factors

- Lack of cooperation between faculty and administration
- Teacher silence
- Demands without voice or explanation
- Presence of security personnel
- Lack of alternative education
- Lack of career preparation
- Inconsistency in rule enforcement
- Apathy about education

Three Levels of Response and Prevention

In the case of violence, prevention steps must be multi-faceted, inter-disciplinary and planned. A good prevention program addresses:

1. Determining what to do as soon as an act of violence occurs.
2. Identifying existing problems after an act of violence.
3. Addressing the underlying causes of violence.

When Violence Occurs

Once an act of violence occurs, certain steps should immediately be set in motion to prevent its escalation. It is of utmost importance to have a comprehensive crisis management plan to follow. A plan limits the damage of violence by providing instructions for direct services to victims.

To prepare for crisis involving violence, select and train the staff to provide the following necessities:

- crisis management
- medical care to those injured and in reactive shock
- protection for students and staff
- information to both the public and the school
- preparation for judicial procedures
- remedial counseling and information to families

Identify Existing Problems

Review the list of factors that promote violence, identify the existing problems, and correct them quickly. This is extremely important because it reduces the chance of violence occurring. It also has a direct bearing on the legal responsibility of the school. If an accident should occur before these problems are solved, the fact that the school has demonstrated an awareness of the problems and has made a sincere effort to rectify them makes the school less legally culpable, even if the problems have not yet been remedied.

Here are some steps you can take immediately to assess the potential for violence and address it.

Counteract denial! Begin with yourself and take a hard look at your institution before someone else does. Ask yourself some probing questions:

- Are aggression and violence escalated or accepted as matter-of-fact?
- Are teachers encouraged to report incidents without fear of reprisal?
- Are students and staff reports held in confidence?
- Are consequences for students delivered with consistency and do they "fit the crime?"

Provide education about violence for both the students and the faculty. Provide alternatives to aggression through conflict resolution, a jury of peers, or negotiation skills training for students.

Promote better relationships between administration, teachers, and support staff. Give voice to dissension and listen. Support your staff and let them know you will back them.

Increase awareness through open discussion. If violence is a growing problem in your school, inviting the staff and student body to participate in creating a safer school environment will generate suggestions, solutions, and support for the mission. Without their input, it is unlikely any program will succeed.

Addressing Underlying Causes of Violence

Primary prevention involves addressing the underlying causes of violence long before they erupt. Some causes are within the school's ability to resolve. Others are not but can be addressed and significantly eased by the school.

Take action with these basic steps:

- Train your staff to be informed, sensitive, and fair to the students growing up in distressful and unwholesome environments.
- Develop a crisis intervention plan and inform your staff and the community that you have it. This increases the trust and faith they place in your school.
- Make necessary physical changes immediately and plan for anticipated improvements.
- Provide alternative educational experiences to increase relevancy for the uninvolved student.

Change attitudes Attitude change is not an easy task and may require a major internal media campaign. An anti-violence emphasis should be included in existing courses and skill-building workshops to decrease victimization should be provided for students needing assistance in:

- Assertiveness
- Leadership
- Self-esteem building
- Anger management
- Conflict resolution
- Self-defense
- Human relations
- Social skills

Role of the Guidance Counselor in Reducing Violence

Guidance counselors have traditionally had minimal involvement in reducing violence since many believe that dealing with violence is the task of the administrators and teachers. They see themselves as consultants and confidantes, as allies to the students, and perceive involvement in disciplinary actions as possibly compromising their ability to help the students.

Counselors are usually not adequately prepared to deal with violence and aggression. Furthermore, schools are prone to dismiss violent or aggressive incidents, placing the blame on aberrant students rather than social problems. Many schools, especially on the secondary level, have their counseling department focus on career and educational counseling without going into social issues or family problems.

Because counselors are the link between family, peer relations, and academics, they are in a unique position to know the whole child and to be far more effective in ferreting out the root of the aggressive behavior than when the behavior is dealt with only through disciplinary action.

Counselors can provide a direct service role by:

- identifying students who experience failure and alienation. These are the students most apt to become violent and aggressive. Students who are unusually excitable, impatient, unrestrained, disrespectful of social norms, or who come from violent homes, can be provided with group counseling. The counseling should address some of the underlying causes of violence—the sense of powerlessness, incompetence and alienation—and concentrate on overcoming anger and frustration in an environment that has a perceived lack of options.

- encouraging students to join clubs and participate in athletics and the performing arts. Help them to discover other activities that promote a sense of involvement with the school community.

- counseling victims about their fear of a second attack and helping them rebuild trust and faith in disciplinary procedure. Advertise the availability of victim support so that any undetected victimization surfaces, allowing for help to be provided.

- identifying students vulnerable to victimization and teaching social skills to the socially isolated, the insecure, the unpopular and the unfamiliar students. Many schools use peer counseling programs to reach these students.

Counselors should sharpen their skills in intercultural relating because they are in an ideal position to impact the problem of escalating aggression in the schools.

In addition to helping students directly, guidance counselors can provide consultation on three levels:

1. Consultation with teachers and professionals. Counselors can conduct training sessions for teachers and interested staff. The focus could be on modeling, role-playing, feedback, and student training. Teachers can then instruct students about how to avoid fights, deal with accusations and provocations, and stay out of trouble with other students.

2. Consultation with parents Because violence in the school is a reflection of the community, involve the community in solving the problem:

- establish a parent network.
- teach parents ways to help students cope without resorting to aggression.
- initiate an Adopt-a-School program through which community organizations can offer assistance to the school (manpower, money, and expertise).
- Begin a Safe-House program.
- Provide restitution programs for early offenders.

3. Consultation with administrators Encourage and help them to:

- monitor hidden corners and courtyards.
- provide opportunities for play and physical release.
- discourage loitering in vulnerable areas.
- encourage retired police officers assigned to the school to be more interactive with the students by talking to them in classes and individually.

COPING WITH A VIOLENT CRISIS

Widespread Effects of a Violent Crisis

We have already discussed certain factors that increase the number of people affected by a crisis. Almost all these factors are present and operating when the violent crisis occurs within a school.

1. A strongly affiliated community—schools work hard to develop this feeling of affiliation, or school spirit.

2. Multiple eye witnesses—almost everywhere in a school facility there is a high density of people, increasing the likelihood that any activity will have eye witnesses present.

3. Victims with special significance—the strong identification with peers, especially on the secondary level, places most students in this category. Certain students, school heroines or heroes, have even more significance.

4. Exposure to carnage—violence by definition results in carnage.

5. Numbers of rescue and police personnel—hostile action occurring in a school brings out every available patrol car. Rescue Services will send out backup EMTs to handle the shock effects as well as the injuries.

6. High media interest—violence always attracts the media and when it occurs in a school, the press will not miss the opportunity for a high-impact story.

Three Waves of Reaction

Because of the widespread impact of a violent crisis on the students, staff and community, it is especially important to have a comprehensive crisis management plan in place and ready to go. Another reason why this is vital is that the immediate aftereffects of a violent episode include three intense waves of reaction that can quickly overwhelm your staff.

FIRST, the police and rescue workers arrive en masse. The police will make the decisions necessary to ensure the safety of students and staff, disarm the situation, and begin the investigation. They will also, for a time, hold the press and parents away from the scene.

SECOND, the press arrives. You can expect the media to be relentless with a violent incident.

THIRD, parents who have heard the news (and are often frantic) will begin to converge on the school and call in for information.

Focus on the Students

During all this activity, the school's main focus must be on the students: those who have been involved in the incident, those who were not involved but have heard what happened, and those who are wondering what all the commotion is about. Each group needs to be handled differently. First and foremost, of course, are concerns about their safety and security.

Safety and Security Concerns

Police Are in Charge

Until everyone's safety is guaranteed, the police make the decisions. If a gunman is holding a class hostage, it is not the school's decision to evacuate the other classes. At any moment, the gunman could leave the classroom and if the halls were crowded with children, he might panic and open fire. SWAT teams are far more prepared to know how and when to evacuate classes.

Provide Facility Information

However, it is important for you to provide the police with information about your facility. They will need:

1. A detailed floor plan of your school, showing all entrances, windows, closets, etc.

FLOOR PLAN OF SCHOOL

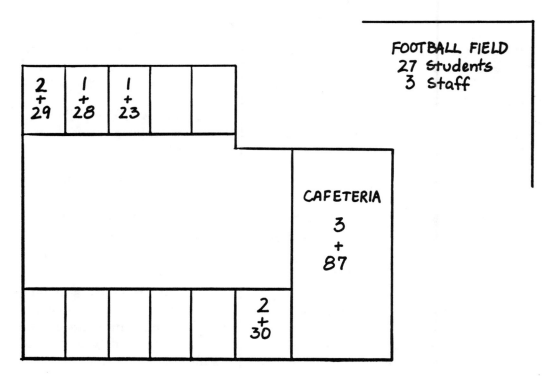

Class Period:

2. Information about where the students are at that moment and the approximate numbers of staff and students.

At the beginning of the semester, reproduce copies of the floor plan for each class period (see example provided). Have the faculty designate where they will be and how many students will be under their supervision at that location for each class period. Include extra-curricular activities if the school is open for use after routine school hours. Keep these floor plans on file in your crisis folder to give to police if the need arises.

The School Determines Dismissal

When the crisis is over, it is the school, not the police, that decides how to dismiss students. In the aftermath of a serious crisis, news has already hit the streets about the incident. Such news can trigger further violent or criminal behavior. Be extraordinarily vigilant for potential negative behavior when releasing students.

While one junior high school was involved with the aftereffects of a tragedy involving a student killed by a drunken driver, a student was called for by an unknown person who waited outside in his car. When the student was released and went outside, he was assailed by the driver and his cohort. Fortunately, the student was able to escape into the school and the car sped away.

Have an Emergency Signal

Establish a signal, usually a coded message over the PA system, which will alert the staff to lock their doors and retain the children. An announcement such as "there will be a meeting after school to discuss the plans for our annual parade" when there is no parade should be understood by all faculty. If an assailant has entered the school, you will want to prevent that person from entering a classroom. It is imperative that all current staff learn the signal. Since acts of violence at the hands of former employees are a growing concern, it might be advantageous to change the signal each year or whenever necessary.

Reassurance about Safety

After such an incident, the school needs a heavy dose of reassurance that all its members are safe. Security procedures may need to be instituted if only for peace of mind. Safety discussions must be held. Adults, especially administrators, need to be very visible to restore the students' trust in the ability of the adult world to protect them. If you cannot increase your staff, enlist community support through volunteer organizations or the PTO. Violent crisis, like other crises, cannot always be prevented or predicted. With a solid plan, however, further violence and chaos can be held to a minimum.

Providing Information

Be Prepared to Answer Calls

The presence of police cars, rescue vehicles, a SWAT team, and the press during a police action will cause a neighborhood commotion and, within minutes, calls will start. Long before any violent action occurs, identify a person on your staff who can handle the calls immediately. Arm him/her with instructions on what to say during an incident, for example:

- "No one is hurt."
- "The police have the situation in hand."
- "We currently have the children under police protection."
- "Do not attempt to come to the school; the police are allowing no one through."
- "You will be notified by the school when you can get your child."
- "The news will keep you informed about when to retrieve your child."

When addressing the media, there is no need to respond to questions about what happened. It is a police matter and only the police can determine which details should be made public. However, in this, as in all instances, the principal must speak to the press about what the school can and will do.

This is when you discuss your crisis plan and invite parents to a debriefing. When questions arise about how a person could get onto the campus, review your policy and safeguards. Acknowledge that you cannot make the school a prison but that you will review all procedures regarding safety and do everything possible to ensure that nothing of this nature happens again.

Helping Students Cope

Students Not Directly Affected

For those students not directly affected, dismissal should come after the announcement is made concerning what happened. You cannot hide the information, because they will hear it on the evening news and it is far better for the principal to speak personally with the students and staff. If parents are waiting, allow them into the school to be with their children and follow whatever method of announcement your crisis team has prepared. Allow a few minutes of defusing to help them ventilate their reaction.

Students Directly Affected

In order to prevent post-traumatic stress disorder, counselors should insure that all students directly affected by a violent incident receive a range of services:

- defusing before dismissal the day of the incident
- debriefing sessions over a period of weeks
- ongoing counseling if needed
- protection from reminders of the incident
- legal assistance

Frequently, in order to save face or support a "tough" image, these students will say they don't need the defusing and debriefing sessions. They do; make these sessions mandatory for all students directly affected. For others, the debriefings (not the defusing session) are optional. However, the students directly affected by the incident should *not* be mixed with any other students for any of the debriefings or you run the risk of increasing the emotionality in the less-affected students. These students do not need to hear the bloody details the directly-affected group has experienced.

The Defusing Session

This is a group no larger than 15-20 people that meets *before* the students or staff leave the premises. A parent who has arrived may sit in if the child wishes. The defusing is essentially no more than talking about what happened, where each person was during the event, listening to all the emotional reactions and letting the participants know that it is normal to experience this kind of reaction. People at this time are too much in shock to really explore their feelings or make sense of the situation. They are to be listened to and comforted.

Debriefing

The debriefing consists of a series of group meetings over a period of time. The first meeting usually occurs within a few days of the incident, the second a week later, the third in about two weeks, followed by one in a month. They are gradually spaced further apart. Normally four to six meetings are needed.

In the debriefing, the counselor begins by discussing the event and then moves on to how the event has changed things in the participants' lives. The students are then asked how they feel about these changes and the event itself. The responses will be highly emotional. After the emotions have been expressed, the counselor should begin to bring the group back to information processing, focusing on what each individual is doing to cope with these feelings. The counselor should encourage their support and identification with one another. Reassurance about how well they are doing and recognition of their strengths conclude the debriefing.

During the second and third round of debriefings, the students may wish to avoid a painful memory. Facing the pain now, however, will reduce the amount of pain overall for a long time. Remember that Post Traumatic Stress Disorder is no more than a delayed reaction to trauma that becomes more severe because it is delayed. The reason for holding the debriefings is to prevent this severe future reaction.

Ongoing Counseling for Some

Ongoing individual or group counseling is essential for two types of students:

1. high-risk students, whether they were directly affected by the incident or not. Violence breeds violence and it is these students who are more likely to react with their own brand of violence after one incident has already occurred.
2. intensely involved students—those most immediately affected by the incident.

Reducing Reminders

When children have experienced violence in a certain location they should not have to be explosed again to the place as it was. A classroom should be changed, even if it has to be switched with one housing the least affected students. The room should be repainted and rearranged before any class meets there. Schedules may need to be changed. The goal of these changes is to reduce familiar reminders of the incident especially for those students who had been involved.

Legal Assistance

Provide ongoing instructions for students and parents of those who will be involved in giving testimony or depositions. Use your local guardian ad litem program to help children through depositions. The District Attorney can instruct and reassure parents and students, while the National Organization for Victim Assistance office can provide information and support.

Support for the Staff

Before the day is over, the staff will need the same attention as prescribed for the students. In one city, an incident occurred where a gunman unloaded his semi-automatic rifle on an office of seventy employees. Nine were killed and three were injured. The rest viewed the bloody scene, hiding under desks. The usual rate of employee retention after such an incident is 40%. This corporation, very responsive to the emotional needs of its employees, followed the guidelines we have outlined and, six months later had retained 90% of the employees affected. You must offer the same service to your staff.

COPING WITH A NATURAL DISASTER

Natural disasters usually cause community-wide devastation. The inflicted damage is sudden, irreversible and widespread. During the turmoil of a hurricane, tornado, earthquake, flashfire or flood, individuals know their familiar world no longer exists and that they are in danger and out of control. Within the actual disaster area, communication systems invariably break down, further isolating the victims.

Sense of Control Devastated

With most other tragedies, people can learn, in retrospect, which precautions and preventive actions should be taken to avoid or decrease negative impact. By reviewing their actions and taking corrective measures to reduce the likelihood of future occurrences, they regain a sense of control and mastery over their lives.

Unfortunately, this approach doesn't work with natural disasters. No one can prevent such an occurrence and even long after one has taken place, the victims must acknowledge that they cannot avoid the possibility of a similar devastation in the future. To the survivor of a natural disaster, nature will forever be understood as both beauty and beast.

Factors Affecting Recovery

The personal lack of control and the widespread destruction inherent in most natural disasters are the two factors that make recovery especially difficult. Reports of any current calamity will kindle a resurgence of fear.

When the San Francisco earthquake occurred in 1990, relatively close on the heels of Hurricane Hugo, news reports in Charleston compared it to Charleston's major destructive earthquake at the turn of the century, thereby triggering, once again, Charleston's realization of its vulnerability. Having just lost lives and property through Hurricane Hugo, the South Carolina city experienced a resurgence of fear and anxiety among the storm's victims.

Other factors detrimental to recovery from natural disasters include:

- loss of irreplaceable family possessions (wedding pictures, gifts, personal memorabilia).
- multiple relocations and time spent in public shelters.
- inadequate financial restitution for losses.
- mass media coverage (if the reporters are able to penetrate the disaster area) and, the resulting invasion of privacy and incorrect reporting.

Recovery from natural diaster loss is a lengthy process which requires 1) the satisfaction of emotional and financial losses, 2) an ability to give a meaning to the disaster, and 3) the individual's capability to cope with long-term stress.

Problems Specific to Natural Disasters

When a natural disaster hits, there is usually an accompanying disruption in communication systems and this serves only to intensify, for the victims, the sense that the entire world has become unglued. In the aftermath of Hurricane Hugo, the television and radio stations of Charleston were damaged and people within the path of the hurricane had no information beyond what they could see. What they saw was utter destruction.

For those who remain in the area hit by a natural disaster, telephone communication will probably be disrupted, leaving family and friends to worry about one another's safety and whereabouts. Access to the hardest-hit areas is limited, thus blocking out food, water, shelter provisions and medical personnel. For those who have evacuated, there may be no way to regain access to their homes.

Looting may occur and often the National Guard is sent to monitor the situation. Because of the lack of supplies, lines form for the essentials and the presence of Guardsmen amid the rampant destruction gives the area the appearance of a war zone. Curfews are usually established. The disruption of electricity will leave a city in unfamiliar darkness with no street or house lights burning. These conditions transform previously safe, comfortable surroundings into a surreal landscape devoid of the familiarity that fosters community and security.

Crisis creates unity, however, and draws aid from many unexpected sources, but whether that aid can reach the affected people or not depends on the disaster. After the San Francisco earthquake, aid was quickly mobilizied, but with Hurricane Hugo the area of devastation was so widespread that it was not possible to immediately get resources to all of the people in need.

Emotional Reactions to Widespread Disaster

The predominant emotional reaction to a natural disaster is fear. Acts of nature strike so suddenly that no one, regardless of how strong, smart or savvy, truly escapes. When the disaster is over, it is extremely difficult to build up a sense of future preparedness because people feel intensely helpless and defeated.

In children and young people, this fear is expressed through general anxiety, hyperactivity, flashbacks, nervousness, undue cautiousness, and, because these children have seen the trauma endanger their families, a separation-anxiety at school. Many people, but especially elementary age children, are prone to illness. In the aftermath of Hurricane Hugo, referrals to nursing clinics increased, mostly for stomachaches and headaches which the nurses felt were psychologically-based.

High schools reported increased truancy. Sometimes this was due to the financial devastation of families which needed their teenagers at home to care for siblings or help provide an income. Those students who had already considered dropping out were now provided the impetus to do so. High–risk families that functioned marginally during normal times were now pushed over the edge, resulting in substance abuse and increased psychiatric hospitalizations. The areas worst hit had the most severe problems as students gravitated to their families rather than to the school.

Post Traumatic Stress Disorder manifested itself in the community by:

1. low-level depression in adults
2. increased illnesses in children and adults
3. truancy in teens
4. an increased level of substance abuse
5. general anxiety.

Anxiety and fear resulting from a natural disaster are emotions easily rekindled by any reminders of a disaster possibly recurring. For example, after a flood or hurricane, a simple rainstorm will remind the victim that it could happen again. This anxiety is usually short-lived. A student who remains anxious several months later is considered at risk for Post Traumatic Stress Disorder.

Implementing a System-Wide Crisis Plan

All the events discussed so far in this book have been crises which strike one school with minimal fall-out to feeder schools. But when a natural disaster strikes, the entire school system may be hit. The crisis plan must consider every school in the system.

Crisis Trainer

In every school, one person, usually a guidance counselor, should be designated as the crisis trainer for that school. This person acts as a resource to

1. assess children who are referred by teachers
2. screen children for further referral
3. advocate for parent involvement when necessary
4. consult with the teachers and the principal.

Students who are beginning to show signs of delayed recovery should be placed in a group conducted by the in-school crisis trainer.

Team Leader

A natural disaster may cause school problems that involve facility use, staff, programs and individual student attention. To keep this network working effectively, each school's crisis trainer should report to a designated team leader who is the resource person for all trainers from schools in their area. Team leaders do not have direct involvement with staff and students of a particular school but act as advisors and intermediaries to the school board, advocating for the resources needed by their area schools.

System-Wide Crisis Team

When a natural disaster occurs, a system-wide crisis team should be called on or established (see Part I) to provide crisis support directly to students and staff members who require more in-depth help than that offered by the school trainer. This team usually comprises board-based and well trained student services personnel whose job it is to respond to emergencies with consultation and counseling. These professionals must decide whether the school system resources are sufficient for the ongoing recovery of the students referred or whether they must be referred to community mental health facilities.

REFERRAL SYSTEM FOR STUDENTS AFTER A NATURAL DISASTER

Teacher in Class

- Addresses all the students using activities and discussions
- Identifies children with problems

Crisis Trainer for School

- Usually a Counselor
- Provides screening and supportive counseling for problem students
- Refers serious problems to team leader

Team Leader for Area Schools

- Orchestrates services between school system and individual schools

Crisis Team for System

- Usually a social worker or psychologist
- Provides in-depth short-term counseling and further screening

Community Mental Health

- Addresses psychiatric problems and students requiring long-term counseling

Teachers Need Time and Attention

Adequate time and attention must be given to the educators who must help the students. The teachers and counselors also feel the aftereffects of the disaster and may have themselves lost homes and loved ones. Recalling them to school several days before the students return is necessary to provide the time for support and contact among co-workers. Since natural disasters usually strike communication systems, these members of the faculty may not have been in touch with one another.

The second purpose for giving teachers time is to prepare them to anticipate certain behaviors from the students. They will need to review the recommended activities and be instructed on the identification and referral procedures for distressed students.

Teachers also need time to ready their classrooms for the return of the students. It is unlikely that the school building will have remained untouched in a community wrought with havoc; the rooms may be in disarray and facility changes may be necessary. If a wing of a school is destroyed, for example, classes may be doubled, rooms changed and common areas adapted to be classrooms.

Since victims are so emotionally overwhelmed and overworked from the clean-up, this extra time will be extremely helpful for organizing rooms, procedures, activities and thoughts. To prepare the staff to support so many fearful young people for a long time, it is essential to restore their sense of control; these few days will provide the time necessary to do that.

Clean-Up Activities Help Students Recover

If each school has followed the planning to this point, the activities for faculty and counselors will be in place, since they are similar to those for any other crisis. To help, however, with the difficult task of re-establishing a sense of control after a natural disaster, equal attention must be given to the clean-up activities.

One teacher in Charleston brought pre-cut wood and nails to her class. In the days that followed her students constructed birdhouses to replace the nests destroyed when thousands of trees were felled by the hurricane. This exercise gave the children responsibilities similar to those of their parents in rebuilding their own homes. Their activities helped them to "make things right."

WHEN THERE IS A DYING CHILD IN A CLASSROOM

Tommy was a nine-year old victim of leukemia. He was in the third grade, and had missed a lot of school in the two years his illness had been developing. Now he was missing school regularly on the day or two a week he needed to take his treatments. On his good days, Tommy could only attend school in the morning due to fatigue. He had lost his hair and eyebrows. His sickly appearance had many students questioning what was going on. It was at this point that the school sought outside consultation.

Sometimes it is questioned whether a child so sick and bearing this serious a prognosis should be attending school at all. It is a well-intentioned question from concerned adults. The answer is yes, the child should be attending. A child may be dying but is also still living and wants to do all the things any child wants to do: play, learn, and be with friends. Just because a child may be facing something that we, as adults, have tremendous difficulty with, he is still a child. A sick child is no more interested in activities or concepts beyond his developmental age than is any other child. All the diliemmas of that particular age are still present.

An adolescent who has lost her hair and may be losing her life is still concerned about how she looks, whether her friends will reject her and whether she will finish her treatment in time for the game on Friday. However, this does not mean she is unaware of her condition. She is aware of her impending death but typically, as a child, is less afraid of death than adults. The child's concern could easily be how the adults around her will recover.

Because the progression of disease in children is more difficult to predict than in adults, hope remains an integral part of the picture until very near the end. Parents need to maintain hope to sustain themselves through the caretaking they must give because it is incredibly difficult for them to watch their child undergo the pain of treatment and slowly succumb to disease.

Death may be imminent, but the parents can hold on to hope so tightly that the school may be unable to prepare the other students. Medical information is confidential and any information given out must meet with the approval of the child's parents. Not infrequently is a school caught in this dilemma. But there *is* a way out. First, every effort should be made to obtain the parents' permission to speak to the students factually about the child's condition. If this should prove unsuccessful, the following format may be used even if the school does not have parental permission to address the issue of death.

Addressing the Issue of Death

Having the student present will hamper classmates from asking the questions they really need to have answered. They will all be hesitant to upset the child, even if the child has expressed an ability to handle the discussion. Address the issue at a time when the student is absent, or send the student on an errand.

Begin by discussing what the students have noticed aobut their fellow classmate. This gives you some idea what thoughts are on their minds and gets them used to speaking about such a sensitive issue. Gradually lead into the fact that the student is very ill. Then begin to get the students' opinions about the illness.

At this point, it is essential to discuss how this student's illness is different from the everyday illnesses to which they are all susceptible. The younger the children, the greater the fear will be that they may also get that sick.

Ask if anyone believes they can "catch" the illness from the student.

The reassurance you give them now must be repeated often to keep their fears alleviated. The younger the child, the less their understanding of illness and how illness occurs. They will need to be reassured as often as necessary to subdue their fear.

Lead the students into discussing what may happen to their classmate. When a child has been very sick, students will be concerned about his possible death. The way to respond is that we never know exactly when someone will die. All we know is that the student is very, very sick with a disease from which some people do die. If you have permission from the parents, discuss the reality: "The doctors think there is a good chance he might die."

When the conversation gets to this point, it is also essential to have students discuss what happens when a person dies. Reassure them that everyone is making the ill child's time here as happy as possible and that the class will learn how to help him and each other through this sad time. Allow discussion to continue, including occasional periods of silence, so that all the questions surface and all the children have the opportunity to have their concerns addressed.

To uplift the mood, start a discussion of all the nice things they appreciate about their ill classmate. Ask them about funny events they remember until most of them are lively and smiling.

To empower the students, begin to discuss things they can do that will make the time with their classmate a happier time. In this discussion, be very directive with the students, reinforcing and planning for the appropriate suggestions and curtailing the inappropriate ideas.

Since the emotional energy level will be very high at this point, steer this energy into an activity to release their emotions: collectively draw a giant class card, compose a poem or a song together, record and send it to the student, or plan and begin a project for the student.

In closing, remind the students about whom they can talk to whenever they wish about the day's discussion and that they will all be learning how to provide a circle of love and caring for their classmate.

After such a session with the class, the topic should be brought up periodically to encourage conversation so that no child is left wondering in isolation. Actively remind students of and direct them toward tasks that show compassion and understanding of the sick child. If the young students feel they have contributed to his well-being, there will be far less guilt and remorse to deal with after his death.

When the dying child is in elementary school, much more work needs to be done with classmates over a longer period of time. The work can be concentrated in the child's class, however, and does not necessarily need to be addressed school-wide. If the student is in junior high or high school, however, the issue may have to be discussed in several classes or on several grade levels, because the network of contacts is greater and the propensity for emotional reactions is heightened.

The Need to Dispell Rumors

Discussion at the secondary level is essential to dispel rumors about the disease. Enabling the students to understand the disease process prepares them in a way that will allow them to show their natural sympathy. Help them to understand that, more than anything else, the dying students wants to be normal and wants to be treated as normally as possible.

One student, a young girl of sixteen, was dying of bone cancer. When the disease process began to show and her body was emaciated from her chemotherapy treatments, rumor spread through her high school that she was dying of AIDS. The girl was so embarrassed that, despite her ability to attend school, she requested to be placed on home-bound status. Her request was granted and, because her mother worked, this young girl spent her dying days alone at home. This tragic situation could have been prevented had a simple plan of action been in place.

In contrast, a twelfth-grader, dying of Hodgkins disease, wanted especially to graduate with the classmates with whom he had shared his school years. The students were informed about the disease as well as the needs of the young man and, although he didn't live to graduate with his classmates, he was provided a graduation ceremony in which he received his diploma. He died shortly after, surrounded by friends and teachers who understood and had included him in their lives and activities.

No plan conceived will ever be perfect and cover all situations equally well but the absence of a plan is often the cause of devastating results. The importance of a cohesive and comprehensive plan is readily seen in the deaths of these two young people.

APPENDIX

BOOKS FOR STUDENTS

Primary Grade Level

Alexander, Sue, *NADIA THE WILLFUL*, New York: Pantheon Books, 1983.

> Willful Nadia's favorite brother dies and her father decrees that no one can talk about him. This book emphasizes how important it is for one to talk about death and the life of the deceased.

Anders, Rebecca, *A LOOK AT DEATH*, Minneapolis, Minn: Lerner Publications, 1978.

> This book describes the sadness that comes of death and the importance of mourning. It is compassionate and positive.

Bartoli, J., *NANNA*, New York: Harvey House, 1975.

> This book demonstrates the patience and understanding needed by young children through the death of a young boy's grandmother.

Bernstein, Joanne E., *WHEN PEOPLE DIE*, New York: Dutton, 1977.

> This book answers with assurance the many questions on children's minds after a death.

Brown, Margaret, *THE DEAD BIRD*, Reading, Ma.: Addison-Wesley, 1965.

> This classic book describes the reactions of a group of young children as they find a dead bird.

Carrick, Carol, *THE ACCIDENT*, New York: Seabury Press, 1976.

> Christopher witnesses the accidental death of his dog. He goes through the grief process rehearsing trying to find ways to undo the accident until he reaches acceptance of the death.

DePaola, Tomie, *NANA UPSTAIRS AND NANA DOWNSTAIRS*, Middlesex, England: Penguin Books, Ltd. 1973

> This book deals on a very simple level with concepts of death through the death of a great-grandmother and the impending death of a grandmother.

Fassler, Joan, *MY GRANDPA DIED TODAY*, New York: Human Science Press, Inc., 1971.

> This is an illustrated book about a young child's reactions to the death of his grandfather.

Herriott, James, *THE CHRISTMAS DAY KITTEN*, New York: St. Martin's Press, 1986.

> This book beautifully describes a relationship between a dying cat and its owner. A time span of a year shows the healing that comes with time.

Kantrowitz, Mildred, *WHEN VIOLET DIED*, New York: Parent's Magazine, 1973.

> This book shows through the death of a bird how very important a ceremony is in accepting death.

Sanford, Doris, *IT MUST HURT A LOT: A CHILD'S BOOK ABOUT DEATH*, Portland, Oregon: Multnomah Press., 1985.

> When a little boy's dog is killed by a car, he experiences grief and loneliness. This book discusses his feelings and the outcomes. It includes instructions for adults using this book with children.

Viorst, Judith, *THE TENTH GOOD THING ABOUT BARNEY*, New York: Atheneum, 1971.

> Through remembering all the good things about his deceased cat, this boy learns to accept death as a reality of life.

Wright, Betty, *MY NEW MOM AND ME*, Milwaukee: Raintree Children's Books, 1981.

> This book sensitively explores through conversations with a cat the reactions to a death of a mother and the arrival of a new mother two years later.

Zolotow, Charlotte, *MY GRANDSON LEW,* New York: Harper, 1974.

This book shows how a young boy lessens his loneliness over the death of his grandfather through sharing the memories.

Upper Elementary Grade Level

Anderson, Leone Castell, *IT'S OK TO CRY,* Elgin, IL: The Child's World, 1979.

The death of an uncle creates discussion between two boys about their feelings, funerals and what happens after death.

Bunting, Eve, *THE HAPPY FUNERAL,* New York: Harper and Row, 1982.

Through the preparation of her grandfather's funeral a young Chinese girl learns to come to terms with her own grief and the comfort of her cultural rituals.

Byars, B., *GOODBY, CHICKEN LITTLE,* New York: Harper and Row, 1980.

This book depicts an offbeat family providing emotional support for a young boy who is very fearful after the death of both his father and his uncle.

Clardy, Andrea Flech, *DUSTY WAS MY FRIEND: COMING TO TERMS WITH LOSS,* New York: Human Sciences Press, 1984.

This book explores coming to terms with feelings after a friend was killed in a car accident.

Cleaver, Vera and Bill, *GROVER,* Philadelphia, PA: J.B. Lippincott, 1970.

When a dying mother kills herself, a father and his eleven-year-old son struggle with their grief and their relationship.

Donnelly, Elfie, *SO LONG, GRANDPA,* New York: Crown Publishing, 1981.

A young boy copes with his grandfather's expected death due to cancer and his recovery afterwards.

Green, Constance C., *BEAT THE TURTLE DRUM,* New York: The Viking Press, 1976.

This book describes the relationship between two sisters before the death of one. The remaining sister experiences the many reactions common to children: anger, feeling the favored sister has died, and confusion over her parents' reactions to the death. The book details feelings about death and its reactions.

Hegwood, Mamie, *MY FRIEND FISH*, New York: Holt, 1975.

This is the story of a black urban child and his friendship with a fish who dies.

Lee, Virginia, *THE MAGIC MOTH*, New York: Seabury Press, 1972.

This book shows the different reactions of the four surviving children in a family which has losts its middle child.

MacLachlan, Patricia, *SARAH PLAIN AND TALL*, New York: Harper and Row, 1985.

This book describes the father's search for a new wife after this little girl's mother has died. This Newberry Award Winner shows the acceptance and growing love for the new mother.

McLendon, Gloria H., *MY BROTHER JOEY DIED*, New York: Julian Messner Publisher, 1982.

This book covers the gamut of problems resulting from the death of an older brother: guilt, problems in school, the funeral, harsh comments from others. This is a good discussion book.

Miles, Miska, *ANNIE AND THE OLD ONE*, Boston, MA: Little, Brown and Co., 1985.

A story depicting the natural way of life and death to a young Indian girl whose grandmother believes she will die when the rug she is weaving is completed.

Paterson, Katherine, *BRIDGE TO TERABITHIA*, New York: Thomas Y. Crowell Co., 1977.

The imaginary world of two friends ends abruptly in the death of one of the friends. This book, winner of the Newberry Award, sensitively describes the guilt felt by the survivor.

Rofes, Eric E., *THE KIDS BOOK ABOUT DEATH AND DYING*, Boston, MA. Little, Brown and Co., 1985.

This book is a discussion of a students' group exploring the different kinds of death, different emotional reactions, and different approaches to life after death.

Smith, Doris Buchanan, *A TASTE OF BLACKBERRIES*, Elgin, IL.: Chariot Books, 1981.

After a friend dies of a bee sting, this little boy feels guilty and experiences a full range of emotional reactions to the death of a friend.

Stolz, Mary, *THE EDGE OF NEXT YEAR*, New York: Harper and Row, 1974.

> When a boy's mother dies in an auto accident, he is left with a little brother and an alcoholic father. The book demonstrates how different people deal with loss in different ways and provides healing even in the face of hopelessness.

Tolan, S.S., *GRANDPA AND ME*, New York: Scribner's, 1978.

> Eleven-year-old girl speaks candidly about her coping with the increasing senility of her grandfather and his eventual suicide.

Wallace, Bill, *A DOG CALLED KITTY*, New York: Pocket Books, 1980.

> This book demonstrates many losses through the relationship with a dog and its death. This is a good book for generating discussion.

White, E.B., *CHARLOTTE'S WEB*, New York: Harper and Row, 1952.

> A classic story using animals to portray the natural events of life and death.

Zim, Herbert and Sonia Bleeker, *LIFE AND DEATH*, New York: William Morrow and Co, 1980.

> This book provides factual answers to questions about life and death. It deals sensitively with physical facts, attitudes, traditions and feelings.

Teens

Aaron, C., *CATCH CALICO!*, New York: Dutton, 1979.

> This story is about a fourteen-year-old and his grandfather's search for a wildcat. The search ends with the boy having to shoot the cat and deal with his grandfather's death from the cat's rabid bite.

Agee, J. Bantam, 1969 *A DEATH IN THE FAMILY*, New York:

> This Pulitzer Prize winning novel offers incredible insights into the impact of a death on the family and the misunderstandings that occur.

Angell, J., *RONNIE AND ROSEY*, Scarsdale, N.Y.: Bradbury Press, 1977.

> A young suburban adolescent must learn to cope with her family's move and her father's sudden, accidental death.

Arundel, H., *THE BLANKET WORD*, Nashville, TN: Nelson, 1973.

> This book portrays the idealism and self-doubts of a young college student as she finds new meaning in relationships after the death of her mother.

Buck, Pearl S., *THE BIG WAVE,* New York: Lothrop, 1948.

> This novel features a young Japanese fisherman, left to deal with the destruction of his entire village, as he changes his views of life and death.

Donovan, John, *I'LL GET THERE. IT BETTER BE WORTH THE TRIP,* New York: Harper and Row, 1969.

> This book provides a tough, realistic and sensitive look at a young teen who suffers several losses: death of a custodial grandmother, a move to New York City to live with an alcoholic mother in the midst of a divorce, and his dog's death. There is much to learn from his growing up.

Guest, Judith, *ORDINARY PEOPLE,* New York: Ballantine Books, 1980.

> This is the powerful story of a family bereft by unexpressed grief over the death of one son and the attempted suicide of the other son.

Huntsberry, W.E., *THE BIG HANGUP,* New York: Lothrop, 1970.

> This book follows the guilt and grief of young survivors after a friend has been killed in an auto accident involving teenage drinking and driving.

Krementz, Jill, *HOW IT FEELS WHEN A PARENT DIES,* New York, Alfred Knopf, 1981.

> Eighteen children discuss what happened to them when their parent died. Children aged seven to sixteen tell of their feelings about the death and remarriage of the remaining parent. This is a useful resource for teachers and counselors as well.

LeShan, Eda, *LEARNING TO SAY GOODBY—WHEN A PARENT DIES,* New York: Maxmillian, 1976.

> This book about recovery from a parent's death is helpful to both young people and the adults who are helping them.

Rabin, G., *CHANGES,* New York: Harper, 1973.

> A teenage boy must learn to find the courage and strength to deal with the death of his father and the changes it brings to his life: a move, change in lifestyle, and the normal pressures of adolescence.

Richter, Elizabeth., *LOSING SOMEONE YOU LOVE: WHEN A BROTHER OR SISTER DIES,* New York: G.P. Putnam and Sons, 1986.

> Sixteen young people describe their emotions and how they learned to cope with a sibling's death.

RESOURCE BOOKS

Grollman, Earl A., *EXPLAINING DEATH TO CHILDREN*, Boston: Little, Brown and Co., 1980.

This book delivers practical information for parents to help their child understand death through theology psychology, biology and culture.

Dunne, Edward, John McIntosh, and Karen Dunne-Maxim, *SUICIDE AND ITS AFTERMATH: UNDERSTANDING AND COUNSELING THE SUR-VIVORS,* New York: W.W. Norton and Co., 1987.

This book offers a comprehensive collection of essays addressing many perspectives of the survivors of suicide, with special chapters devoted to sibling survival and adolescent suicides.

Hughes, P.R., *DYING IS DIFFERENT,* Mahomete, IL: Mech Mentor Education, 1978.

This book promotes discussion about the differences between life and death and the feelings and rituals necessary for recovery.

Marsoli, Lisa Ann, *THINGS TO KNOW ABOUT DEATH AND DYING,* Morristown, NJ: Silver Burdett Co.

Information is given on twenty-five different aspects of death: pets, wills, suicide, hospice, physical death and funerals, to name a few.

Rudolph, Margarita, *SHOULD THE CHILDREN KNOW?* New York: Schocken Books, 1978.

This books speaks sensitively of children's concerns and fantasies, suggesting honest sharing and ways to help young children.

Stein, Sara D., *ABOUT DYING: AN OPEN FAMILY BOOK FOR CHILDREN AND PARENTS TOGETHER,* New York: Walker and Co., 1984.

A text is included for parents to read before reading the book with children. This book provides guidelines to assist parents and children when discussing feelings and actions related to any death.

Wolf, Anna, *HELPING YOUNG CHILDREN TO UNDERSTAND DEATH,* New York: Child Study Press, 1978

This book presents typical questions frequently asked by children with constructive suggestions for family and school discussions.

BIBLIOGRAPHY

Baldwin, A.A. A paradigm for the classification of emotional crisis: Implications for crisis intervention. *American Journal of Orthopsychiatry,* 1978, *48,* 538–551.

Ellis, Albert, *A Guide to Rational Thinking,* Englewood Cliffs, NJ: Prentice-Hall, Inc. 1975.

Erickson, Erik. *Childhood and Society* (second edition). New York, NY: W.W. Norton, 1963.

Gould, M. & Shaffer, D. The impact of suicide in television movies: evidence of imitation. *New England Journal of Medicine,* 1986, 315, 690–694.

Hollar, Cleve Cordell. *Adolescent suicide: the role of the public school.* University of North Carolina at Greensboro, 1987.

Phillips, D. Suicide, motor vehicle fatalities, and the mass media: evidence toward a theory of suggestion. *American Journal of Suicidology,* 1979, 84, 1150–1174.

Report of the Secretary's Task Force on Youth Suicide. US Department of Health and Human Services, 1989, 3:

Bolton, Iris. Perspectives of youth on preventive intervention strategies. pp. 264–275.

Felner, R. Primary prevention: a consideration of general principles and findings for the prevention of youth suicide. pp. 23–30.

Shaffer, D. & Bacon, K. A critical review of preventive intervention efforts in suicide, with particular reference to youth suicide. pp. 31–61.

Tanney, Bryan. Preventing suicide by improving the competency of caregivers. pp. 213–224

Vieland, Veronica. School suicide prevention programs: How effective are they? *School Safety and Security Management,* April 1989, 9–14.

Index